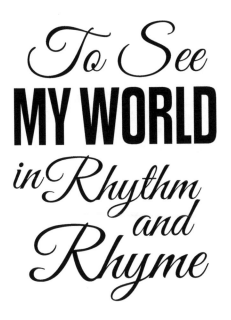

To See MY WORLD in Rhythm and Rhyme

THOMAS WAYNE ALLEN

authorHOUSE®

AuthorHouse™
1663 Liberty Drive
Bloomington, IN 47403
www.authorhouse.com
Phone: 1-800-839-8640

Published by AuthorHouse   11/05/2014

ISBN: 978-1-4969-3505-2 (sc)
ISBN: 978-1-4969-3504-5 (hc)
ISBN: 978-1-4969-3503-8 (e)

Library of Congress Control Number: 2014914701

CONTENTS

SOME THOUGHTS, FACTS, AND MAYBE SOME LIES

UGLY

There were thirty-some kids in my grade school class
And I was the ugliest one.
Whenever anyone looked at me
They'd have to poke some fun.
Ugly wasn't my only problem,
I was also very short.
Fighting wasn't a promising option,
So I learned to be a good sport.
With fire-engine red hair and freckles
It's a good thing I wasn't too moody,
For it didn't take those rascals long
To nickname me "Howdy Doody."
Just to give you an idea of how ugly;
My teacher, ol' Mrs. Long,
Would make me stand with my nose in the corner
When I hadn't done anything wrong.
Then puberty hit me downright hard
And those girls were really lookin' good.
I thought, "Who could kiss a mug like this?"
And I knew that none of them would.
However, With my vivid imagination
And these feelings I couldn't resist,
I would picture them clearly in my mind
And make passionate love to my fist.
Expecting things to get better as I grew older
I supposed the teasing would eventually be gone.
But this truly ugly duckling
Didn't turn into a swan.
I grew a beard to cover my face,
But that idea didn't work worth a damn.
Instead of "Howdy Doody,"
I was now "Yosemite Sam."

My schooling did prove to be helpful
For I have a sweetheart now.
I devised a plan to make it happen.
Would you like me to tell you how?
I met her on a hazy night,
Actually a really dense fog.
I was able to comfort her with hugs and caresses,
After killing her seeing-eye dog.

HILLBILLY LAW

When you hear us a talkin' 'bout down home,
We're a meanin' up in the hills.
Ya'll think we look silly and call us Hillbilly,
And make fun of us and our stills.

Our lives, no doubt, are simpler than yours,
Seldom ever we get in a hurry.
But it's a real pity when we trek to the city,
That kinfolk down home must worry.

You'uns seem bound to make trouble with us,
When deep down you know it ain't right.
When you mess with us'uns we'll spit out some cussin',
And someone gets hurt in the fight.

Kinfolk amends or kinfolk revenge,
Is somethin' you should try to shun.
Hill-Bills and Hill-Jacks don't take well to wisecracks,
And all of us carry a gun.

We've learned o'er the years through bloodshed and tears,
Fingerprints won't be left at the scene.
To you we all look alike - Billy, Jack or Ike,
And we're dirty and downright mean.

Now when we come to town, don't be messin' around.
Be smart and mind your own biz.
Treat us right and there won't be no fight,
I'm a tellin' you just how it is.

We're seldom convicted of murder.
The courts will throw these cases out.
Prosecutors refuse when they think they will lose.
And with us, there's a reasonable doubt.

Even with the new scientific break-through,
We know we'll get our release.
Hillbillies all have the same DNA,
And none of us have any teeth.

So you honkies-and brothers-and all of you others,
Don't mess with the kinfolk we loves.
For if you do, we'll find you,
And we'll be a wearin' our gloves.

WIFE THINKS I'M LAZY

The wife thinks that I am lazy
And a hypochondriac.
If she hurt the way I hurt,
She wouldn't give me so much flack.
Sometimes I feel like the tires on my truck,
Gettin' bald and all worn out.
My shoes don't even have much tread
And I think I've got the gout.
My back, it aches; my knees they hurt.
Got arthritis in my fingers.
Stomach's bloated, throwed away my belt
And started wearin' red suspenders.
The wife wants me to exercise;
Recommends I walk a mile.
She says, "It would be good for you,
Might even make you smile."
I look at her, she looks at me,
And then she walks away.
Me, bein' the man that I am,
I boldly up and say,
"So you would like for me to smile.-
Well, I'll tell you this for certain;
When you're grittin' your teeth and bitin' your lip,
It's hard to smile, when you're a hurtin'.
It hurts for me to walk across this room
And you want me to walk a mile.
Get me another beer and I'll sit right here,
You know that's more my style.
And change the channel on the TV set."
Then I hear her quote,
"I'm not your slave or servant,
And damn sure not your remote!"

BUSTED AT WORK

As I pulled into the driveway I saw
A worker plop down to rest in the shade.
When he saw me, he jumped up, busy as a bee,
Using the tools of his trade.
I parked my truck and walked over to him
And said, "Go ahead and take a break.
It must be a hundred and three today,
Too damned hot, for goodness sake."
I don't know what makes it happen
But you can be bustin' your ass a workin'
And as soon as you stop to catch your breath,
Someone will bust you for certain.
It happens to me all of the time,
Why does it happen this way?
If the boss could catch us a workin' sometimes
We might get a raise in our pay.

SLEEP TALKING

My sweetheart woke up early
And wanted to talk, much too soon.
I tried to converse while still asleep,
But it went over like a lead balloon.
She'd been a thinkin' 'bout breast implants
And asked if I wanted her to do it,
I mumbled, "I know how to make them bigger,
And there ain't a whole lot to it."
"Just take some toilet tissue every day
And rub it between your jugs."
She asked, "How will that do anything,
Toilet paper and daily rubs?"
"I'm not sure what makes it work,
But I know they will grow huge in time.
And I've got proof that it'll work,
Look in the mirror at your behind."

BUSYBODIES

What is it about so many people
Who feel a need to start some trouble?
Are they so inferior and jealous
That they must try to bust your bubble?
My "good buddy" was a friend, for years on end.
We and our wives developed a family like relationship.
But when he recently passed away,
The connection started sinking like a deflated ship.
Why is it, that so called "do gooders"
Must always start running their mouths.
It's terrible to hear you're being talked about
For staying friends with the surviving spouse.
I am retired, but my wife still works;
She's a few years younger than me.
I continued to stop in as I always had done,
But then had to face the harsh reality.
Because I was over there quite a bit,
Since retirement, this was a part of my life,
Somehow it became obvious to many "big mouths"
That I must be having sex with his wife.
Because of these unfounded rumors,
I thought it best that I stop dropping in.
I'm ashamed for allowing this scandalous talk
To take me away from such a good friend.
Why should I feel like I'm doing something wrong
Because of what some nosey gossiper might say?
I plan to renew my valued friendship, if possible,
And these busybodies had best stay out of my way.

THE LIARS BENCH

In Edenton, when I was a kid,
There was a gathering place in town.
Selling pop, beer, tobacco products, candy;
It was the only gas station around.
The little building held a pot-bellied stove,
A wooden church pew back against the wall,
A round card table set out just a bit,
And some bar stools by the candy stall.
Mornings and evenings it was crowded,
A room full of smoke and tobacco stench,
As the old timers told their stories.
We called it "The Liars Bench."
Now I'm one of the old timers
And I have some stories to tell.
I like to share them with my friends
At the "gathering place" in Newtonsville.
We gather around a long table,
"The Table of Knowledge," we say.
I don't recall any geniuses there,
But it's my favorite part of the day.
Most of my good friends have been leaving
To that "gathering place in the sky."
I wonder---is there a liars bench there?
If not---I wonder why?

THE SLANDERER

Do you know people who brag on themselves,
Constantly patting themselves on the back?
Consistently slandering whoever's not there,
And no one gets any slack.
They must think we're all stupid
When we just listen and stare.
But even I can see they'll do the same to me
When I'm the one who's not there.

HER IDEAL PET

The wife thought that a Yorkshire Terrier
Would be her ideal pet.
So plannin' to earn some brownie points,
I started searchin' the Internet.
I found one that lit up my eyes:
A three year old, very well behaved,
And FREE for just a good home.
Look at the dollars I've saved!
I hurriedly e-mailed some alias John Smith,
And arranged to get the critter.
When I bragged to the wife on what I'd done,
She starts a fussin' and treatin' me bitter.
After hem-hawin' and snortin' around she said,
"I don't want any full grown dog from John Smith.
I want a pup that I can watch grow up.
I want one that I can bond with."
Needless to say she'd picked one out.
I was afraid to ask what it cost.
Knowin' her it'd be an arm and a leg.
Now look at the dollars I've lost!
I e-mailed an apology to Mr. Smith,
For havin' to go back on my word.
But he understood, pretty darn good
How a woman's logic is often absurd.
I took out a loan to get the high dollar pup,
And she was enjoyin' him so well.
But the more he matured, the more he manured,
And the more he was raisin' hell!
When the little gopher chewed up her sofa,
That was all the ol' lady could take.
She chased him around the room, swingin' belt and broom,
But failed to catch him, for goodness sake.
As she was concludin' her cussin' and broodin',
I couldn't help myself from responding,
"Well the puppy survived, he's still alive -
Is that what you call bonding?"

13

HARD WORK AND BORING

My imagination helps me make it
Through the drudgery of the day.
I day-dream that I am somewhere else,
So I can keep on pluggin' away.
I'll get to wishin' I was a fishin',
This hard work should be a crime.
Then I start a thinkin' that I'm a drinkin',
And havin' one hell of a time.
As I'm a grinnin' about my sinnin',
With the pretty little thing next door,
My boss will bring me out of my trance,
And pat me on the back for sure.
He'll say, "This work is hard and boring,
But it's work that needs to be done.
I've only known a few men like you,
Who can do it and appear to have fun."
I just grin and look at him,
Not givin' my secret away.
I never knew those other few
But if I was to guess, I'd say
Their imagination helped them make it
Through the drudgery of this place.
I wonder what they would day-dream about
To put a big grin on their face.

PALEFACE MISTAKES

The early American Indian braves
Have made the paleface look like a jerk.
They would hunt and fish for a livin'
And let their squaws do all the work.
They didn't pay any taxes
And never worried 'bout bills.
They knew how to live off of the land
And would share with each other their skills.
If a couple of bison would feed the whole tribe,
Two is all they would take.
They didn't rob the country of all its resources
Like we have, for heaven's sake.
We're supposed to be much wiser today,
But look what we have done.
We've little time for huntin' and fishin',
Our work keeps us all on the run.
The government is constantly raisin' our taxes
And we've got to keep up with the Jones;
So we spend more money than we have
And pay with high interest loans.
If we had to live off of the land,
Most of us would starve or freeze to death.
And if you're a countin' on your neighbor to share with you,
You'd better not hold your breath.
We've even given our women equal rights.
They have an equal vote.
And heck, there's more of them than us,
And that's bound to sink our boat.
I can see it a comin' plain as day,
They'll eventually be makin' the laws.
They'll vote themselves chiefs and like those Indian braves,
Will treat us like we are their squaws.

GOIN' DEAF

Everybody raises hell with me,
'Cause I am goin' deaf.
Hear very little from my right ear,
Nuttin' from the left.
I had to give up my radio,
And quit watchin' the TV.
The wife and kids will up and leave,
If they're loud enough for me.
My youngest son, he has his fun.
Just a movin' his lips.
I wonder how funny he'd think it'd be,
With my boot between his hips?
Sometimes what is said to me
Ain't just what I hear.
And when I politely answer back,
I often get a sneer.
Like when I was asked about my baseball cards.
"Did you happen to keep those?"
I said, "Sure he should be in the Hall of Fame*",
That everybody knows."
When you speak to me, make it one-on-one.
With no background noise.
Not like at the bowlin' alley,
When I'm out with the boys.
I get tired of saying "huh" or "what",
And "Couldn't hear what you said."
I just listen to 'em mumble,
And grin or nod my head.
Don't know what I'm a noddin' to,
Jest hope they talk right on.
For when they gasp and stare at me
I know I've nodded wrong!

*Pete Rose

WHAT BILLS TO PAY?

Just a sittin' here with my paycheck
A listenin' to the radio.
Tryin' to figure out what bills to pay,
They're all past due, you know.
Credit cards are all maxed out,
The banks won't deal with me.
The kids, they are all ticked off
'Cause we lost our cable TV.
The wife's makin' out a grocery list,
We've got to eat, I guess.
I'm a tryin' to devise a plan
To get us out of this mess.
The lights go out, the radio's dead,
Sittin' in the dark and still;
"I guess we'll eat a little lighter this week,
And pay the 'lectric bill."

THE TIP

We enjoyed a really fine meal
And the service was downright good.
But there were eight of us at the table,
So I'll tip much less than I should.
I'm not really a tight-wad
But the bill is a hundred and sixty bucks.
Add fifteen or twenty percent to that
And, wow, that really sucks!
She's a lookin' for some twenty percent,
But ten bills is all this one will be.
We weren't here much over an hour,
And she shouldn't make more than me!

LOOKIN' OVER MY TELEPHONE BILL

I was lookin' over my telephone bill
Just the other day.
Cost me half again as much for a ten mile call,
Than one, a thousand miles away.
Both calls were for five minutes.
Both were listed with an "E."
The call to my neighbor was seventy-five cents,
The one to Texas just fifty.
Now this don't make much sense to me,
So I want to find out why.
I dial the number listed on my bill,
And listen to the reply.
Press "one" for this, "two" for that,
And "three" for something else.
A recordin' goes on and on,
I start mumblin' to myself.
I listened to all these choices.
Then figured I'd press "three."
Thinkin' someone would pick up the phone
And explain my bill to me.
How are they gonna' justify
Chargin' less for far than near?
The phone, it is now picked up,
But what do you think I hear?
Press "one" for this, "two" for that,
And "three" for something else.
A different recordin' goes on and on,
Now I'm cussin' to myself.
Now in anger I press "five,"
A chance to talk to a real person.
I'm gonna really give 'em hell.
But then things begin to worsen.
The phone is actually ringin'!
Then by another recordin' I'm told,
"Due to the high number of incoming calls
You will have to be put on hold.

Your wait will be about two minutes,
Then one of our reps will speak to you."
I hear this recording repeated
Over and over for an hour or two.
I'm not gonna just hang up,
And I'm not gonna be a quitter.
The more they try to put me off,
The more that I get bitter.
I finally get to speak with someone,
I can't believe my ears.
I ask her about my bill,
And her answer nearly brings me to tears:
"Your long distance rate is ten cents a minute,
Local long distance is fifteen."
"Can you tell me why this is?" I ask.
"It's the screwiest thing I've ever seen."
"We're not your long distance service,
For your convenience we handle their billing.
I can give you their eight hundred number,
And you can call them if you're willing."
Again thinkin' to myself,
I'll hear press "one" for this, "two" for that,
And "three" for something else.
I get another recordin',
But this one really gets to me.
I can't understand a word of it,
Until "for English now press 'three.'"

Well I go ahead and press the button,
Dazed and disgusted with myself.
And hear press "one" for this, "two" for that
And "three" for something else.
They keep tryin' to put me off.
I'm feelin' like a fool.
I guess these companies graduated
From the "They'll Get Tired of Waitin' School."
But I hang in there, not givin' up.
I've wasted most of the day.
I still want to know how they justify
Chargin' more for close than far away.
I finally hear a human voice,
At least it could be, from the sound.
I can't understand him very well,
And he don't know his ass from a hole in the ground.
I guess he's tryin' to speak English,
But he's not doin' too well.
I say, "I'm havin' a hard time understandin' you."
So then he begins to yell!
Is this what we've got to look forward to,
with all this talk of global biz?
After waitin' all this time, his answer to me:
"Dat's jest de way it tis!"

YOU'RE A MASON

A mason is a skilled worker who builds
By laying substantial units like stone or brick.
He will build only on solid foundations
And can seal them tightly, forever and quick.
Freemasonry uses the same tools and knowledge
To build character in already good men.
Binding ourselves so closely together
That we actually feel we are kin.
Brothers who enjoy helping others,
Especially those who need it the most;
Doing it only because it's the right thing to do,
Expecting nothing - and never to boast.
"Brothers" who may have different religious beliefs,
But most are really good men.
Some churches preach against Masonry,
Tell me, how can this be a sin?
Yes - I am a Mason,
And I display my emblems with pride.
We do keep some secrets among ourselves
But Freemasonry has nothing shameful to hide.
Please give this to anyone putting us down;
They may be located from coast to coast.
We'd like to help them to understand
They're the ones who may need it the most.

AWARDS & WIDOWS NIGHT

A true Masonic brother is special,
He feels no need to get an award.
He likes to help others as much as he can,
Doing and giving more than he can afford.
Even brothers like these must pass on
To meet the "Great Architect" in the sky.
And leave us here with such a big void
We can't help the tears in our eyes.
I would think these brothers might be placed
In stations higher than any on earth.
Some of us took them for granted,
Never realizing their true worth.
But now we notice and miss them so much,
More than we ever expected.
But our loss can't even begin to compare
With what you widows have been subjected.
It's our pleasure to honor you tonight,
And we'd like to do something more.
-----You are truly our sisters, -----
And we want to help you for sure.
Please don't hesitate to ask
When you need a helping hand.
Your brothers have your best interest at heart,
And we'll help you as much as we can.

TRAPPIN' AND ODORS

When I got the urge to trap predators,
I read every book on it I could get.
Bein' careful with human odor was stressed,
Especially around "the set."
Bein' careful to keep so clean and neat
Cost me a whole lot of time.
Good trappers know that "time is money,"
And to waste it is considered a crime.
I've been a trappin' now for quite a while,
And I oughtta write a book of my own.
Most critters are curious about any new smell.
On this subject my knowledge has grown.
I can take a dump right next to my set
And might have a catch the very next day.
They try to figure out what I've been eatin'
And their curiosity will make them pay.
To show you what I'm a talkin' about,
Check out where someone has gutted a deer.
You'll probably find where predators dined
'Cause their appetite conquers their fear.
Deer hunters aren't careful with human odor
When the kill is bein' field dressed.
Still predators will steal this scrumptious meal
No matter how big of a mess.
There is a place to be careful though,
Never get any odd smell on your trap.
It should smell just the same as the area it's in,
Take this to the bank as fact.

And be sure to place your lure or bait
So the critter steps on the trap pan.
Predators are usually a whole lot like me,
They'll go the easiest way they can.
I'm told that my truck stinks to high heaven,
Lots of lures, urines and tainted bait.
I keep some in the cab 'cause it don't bother me,
I'm used to it, for heaven's sake!
I like to pick up hitch-hikers,
I'll let them run about a quarter a mile.
As they jump in, sit down and take a deep breath,
I peel out, look at them and smile.
Then I ask, "Where are ya travelin' to?"
As they're gaggin' from a whiff of my load.
When I play this game, they all answer the same:
"Just let me out at the very next road!"

TRYIN' OUT A NEW RECIPE

We've heard about "The Tortoise and the Hare,"
With persistence the tortoise wins the race.
We thought it was funny that a turtle beat a bunny,
But a turtle always wins in taste.
I've et some really good rabbit
And dined on fine hasenpfeffer.
You don't need to be bright, when a turtle's cooked right,
To know that it tastes a lot better.
Fry it in a skillet to start with,
To give it a real nice crust.
Then put it in a roaster to finish,
Slow cook in the oven is a must.
When it's done right, it's such a delight
To let it just melt in your mouth.
But when it's done wrong, you're a chewin' too long,
And you might even stink up the house.
I'll tell you what I did one time
When a makin' some new turtle soup.
I knew it weren't a smellin' too good,
And heck, it tasted like poop.
I was a tryin' out a new recipe,
Sposedta cook bottom shell and all.
The wife was a bitchin'; I'd smelled up her kitchen,
And she was a goin' to the mall.
Now I know what I'd done wrong,
I'm sure, I'm not just a guessin'.
It don't take a brick to fall on my head, -
I shouldn'ta cooked that intestine.

THE MASTER DEER HUNTER

I'd bragged at work for months on end
That I was "the master deer hunter."
"No doubt!" I'd say, "I'll get one first day."
For I knew that I had their number.
Was in the woods before day-break,
I'd already picked a good spot.
Plenty of scrapes, rubs, and chewed-up shrubs,
For sure it had to be hot!
I heard some snortin' and movin' around
As I was a climbin' the tree.
Hadn't even opened my lure bottle yet
But I could smell "doe in heat" pee.
Must have been in my stand too early,
Still dark when I heard the deer scatter.
I got so gosh darn cold up there,
My teeth couldn't help but chatter.
I knew I'd caused them to run away
And I'm supposed to know better.
Now I fear that at work I'll hear,
"No kill for the master deer getter?"
At sun-up I got rid of my chill,
Turned out to be a nice day.
I'm not gonna leave, got tricks up my sleeve,
I'll get me a deer anyway.
I rattled some antlers that I'd brought along,
Imitatin' two bucks in a fight.
When they hear this and smell doe in heat piss,
They'll come a runnin' to me day or night.
Well, I feel like a jerk when this don't work,
So I start a snortin' with my buck call.
A buck will snort to fight or court,
And when this fails, I could bawl.
No matter what I did, it was in vain.
I'd tried every trick in the book.
I finally decided to sit back and rest,
It's best to just listen and look.

Didn't leave my stand at all that day,
Was up there twelve hours or so.
I would sprinkle the lure that I had bought
To cover the scent of my yellow snow.
I sat right there a way up in the air,
No food - not even a beer.
Squirrels and chipmunks all over the place,
But not even a glimpse of a deer.
It's almost dark and I'm gonna give up
When I hear some thrashin' and crashin' around.
And to my surprise right before my eyes,
A monstrous buck with his nose to the ground.
He's right under my tree a sniffin' that pee,
And my heart was a beatin' in thumps.
I ease my gun to point it straight down;
My throat was choked with lumps.
I take careful aim for the vital spot
And squeeze the trigger, "*click*", I'm done.
I want to cry, but I'll make up a big lie.
I forgot to put shells in my gun.

A STROKE OF BAD LUCK

I wake up and don't know where I am,
But find myself in a hospital bed.
Cords and IV plugged into me,
And I'm hungry and need to be fed.
I try to holler for a nurse,
But hell, I can't even talk.
Then a bowel movement hits me hard
And all I can do is gawk.
Finally a nurse does come in
To bathe me and clean up my shit.
She says the IV is feeding me
But my stomach just doesn't know it.
Friends and loved ones come to visit
And have lots of questions to ask.
But their requests get me depressed,
Trying to answer is an arduous task.
I'm doing my best to get out of here,
For I darn sure need a smoke.
I'm telling you sis, you don't want none of this.
It's no fun to have a stroke.

MY SQUIRREL RECIPE

Now with fall approachin'
It seems I just can't wait,
To cook up a mess of squirrel
And really fill up my plate.
Some of my friends won't even try it,
They say, "I couldn't eat that.
The squirrel is from the rodent family,
It would be like eating a rat."
When I hear such a stupid statement,
I always spit out some cuss words.
Can you compare the Colonel's chicken,
To a cooked up bunch of buzzards?
So much for that, I'd better go on
And tell you how to do it.
I can make them melt in your mouth
And there ain't a whole lot to it.
First you trap or shoot the critters,
Or hit 'em with your car.
Try not to smash 'em up too bad;
I don't care for the taste of tar.
Now you take each one and skin it,
I mean skin the head, too.
There are several ways to do it,
Do whatever works for you.
With a sharp knife split the pelvic bone,
Make a thin cut from there through chest.
Make sure you don't ever cut too deep
Or you will have a stinkin' mess.
Don't cut, but pull out the innards
And pitch 'em with skin and tail.
Cut the rest into serving size pieces
And put 'em in a water pail.

Slosh 'em around in the water
To clean 'em up a bit.
Now change the water and slosh 'em again,
To wash off all the blood, hair and shit.
You should now have seven pieces:
Four legs, head, chest and back.
Now roll 'em good in flour,
Or shake 'em up with flour in a sack.
Fry it the same as chicken
And season to your taste.
Some throw away the squirrel's head,
But that's a terrible waste.
The jaw meat is soft and tender,
Just bite 'em off first thing.
Then squeeze the skull and crack it,
Try not to damage the brain.
The brain will come out all in one piece,
Don't stop; you're still not done.
Take the teeth and pull the jaw apart
To get that delicious tongue.
I better put my pencil down,
By now you think I'm weird.
I also make squirrel gravy
But it's hard to keep out of my beard.
One thing I forgot - when dressin' a squirrel,
Be sure to cut out its eyes.
You don't want the thing a lookin' at you
From the skillet while it fries.

OLD TALES

I've always enjoyed listenin' to old timers,
A stretchin' the truth when the opportunity occurs.
They have a knack, when they remember back,
To take more credit than they deserve.
Most will start out with true memories,
But o'er the years have added somethin' new.
After tellin' the same lies long enough,
They eventually believe that they're true.
You'd better not question or doubt 'em,
Or you'll be written off as a friend.
They can't tolerate thinkin' they told you a lie,
And will swear that it's true to the end.
I've even noticed myself, after tippin' a few,
And a startin' to feel a good buzz,
When a tellin' some old tales of my own,
The older I get, the better I was.

ADVICE TO HEED

(But you think you don't need)

A CARDINAL LIFE

While putting some thoughts together
I was rudely interrupted today
By a bird flying against my window
In a very peculiar way.
The male cardinal would hit the solid glass,
Striking it time and time again.
Not showing much wit, he just wouldn't quit;
Reminds me of you young men.
You try to get next to the opposite sex
By putting down your perceived competition.
Doing whatever it takes, making huge mistakes,
Sometimes resulting in self demolition.
You'll pick a fight when you know it's not right,
If you could only see how stupid you look.
I believe you'd try harder to do things smarter
And get yourself off of this hook.
I noticed in the cardinal's actions today,
Your thinking was shown to perfection.
When this handsome red bird looked rather absurd
Attacking his own reflection.
I'm sure he's a legend in his own mind
As he puts himself through all of the pain.
Young man, it's not cool to act like a fool.
Grow up and don't be a bird brain.

KINDNESS

Kindness develops into happiness;
Harshness hurts and is so offensive.
Kind words cost nothing to give,
While harsh ones can be expensive.
Do you frequently argue with those you love?
Grossly spitting out whatever would hurt,
Cussing and fighting like thunder and lightning,
Inevitably creating more dirt?
If you're doing this, you'd better change,
I hope you can use this to remind you.
Harsh love is brittle and eventually breaks;
Put this way of living behind you.
How important is winning an argument?
Is it worth losing a loved one?
Proving you're right to win the fight,
Then later regretting what you've done.
Be kind and gentle to those you love,
Never permit anger to steer you.
Show no blindness to true kindness
And all will want to be near you.
Whenever a loved one upsets you,
It's a given - for certain they will,
Take a deep breath to settle down
And just for a bit-"Keep Still."
It's O.K. to have your say,
In fact you should be the example.
You must feel free to disagree
But do it in a way that is ample.
Speaking kindly to a loved one who hurts you
Doesn't mean that you're meek or weak.
But it can show- "that you do care."
Be kind - and think before you speak.

DROWNING SORROWS

Do you remember when you were so happy
When you found "the love of your life?"
The whole word changed with your life rearranged
And you became husband and wife.
With fine careers developing,
You invest in a really nice house.
The future is looking "oh, so good"
For you and your loving spouse.
To climb that ladder of success
Takes so much planning and thinking.
To rub noses with those who might be of help,
You indulge in social drinking.
The trouble with drinking socially
Is that you quickly acquire a taste for it.
Keeping your own supply at home,
Designating a convenient place for it.
The world's again changing and your life's rearranging,
And it's not looking quite so good.
You're drinking very frequently now,
Taking in more booze than you should.
When alcohol takes control of you,
If it hasn't, you know that it will,
That ladder of success may fall and break.
And whose love do you think it will kill?
Only one of you is working now
And the economy is getting worse.
Please lighten up on what goes in your cup,
Ridding yourself of this curse.
I'm worried about "my dear friend,"
What's going to happen to you?
Drowning your sorrows doesn't make good tomorrows;
Plan and think right now what to do.

TWIN BRIDGES

When I was young and thinking dumb,
I tried to have others believe
That I was much braver than I was,
Showing utter stupidity to deceive.
I was a loudmouth and show-off,
Doing most anything to get attention.
Even putting my life at risk;
I've picked just one here to mention.
I was set up by so-called "friends"
Who felt my showing off was brimming.
Thinking that they would teach me a lesson
Taking me along to go swimming.
Twin Bridges is where they took me.
"Dave dives from the top of the highest one.
It's about a hundred foot dive to the river.
Don't you think that would be fun?"
I said, "Boy that sounds exciting."
Knowing I've never done any diving before
But if Dave can do it and it don't hurt him,
I can certainly do it for sure.
I climbed up, with Dave, to the very top
And watched him "swan dive" off like a pro.
He made it look so graceful and easy;
He put on an impressive show.
He glided like a bird with his arms wide open
Then drew them together to enter.
He quickly shot back up to the surface,
And motioned for me to dive to the center.
As I gasped at the distance down to the water,
I discovered my great fear of heights.
I figured I'd die if I gave this a try,
But being seen as a coward bites.

So I took a deep breath and held it,
Leaned forward to make my dive.
As I hit the air came a terrible scare
For none of my senses would jive.
I wanted to watch as I went down,
But from panic my eyes locked shut.
It seemed like I fell for a lengthy spell,
Stiff from fear - head, limbs, chest and gut.
When I finally slammed into the river,
It felt like my head was struck with a board.
I shot like a bullet straight to the bottom,
Somersaulting on rocks was my reward.
Realizing I'm alive and not seriously hurt
Was a wonderful sense of relief.
I'd escaped instant death, but was now out of breath
So my pleasant feeling was brief.
I was thirty feet down and thought I would drown;
Apparently swimming I'd not fully learned.
I paddled with fury to reach the top in a hurry;
Held my breath but my lungs really burned.
I finally broke water, took in some deep breaths,
And slowly swam o'er to shore,
Pretended that this was no big deal,
But I knew I'd never do that anymore!
Dave said, "Shall we do it again?"
I replied, "Sure there's lots of excitement to it,
But before we do - I'd like to -
Watch these other guys do it."

I wonder how many tragedies
Have caused loved ones to suffer gravely,
Because someone young was thinking dumb,
And perished - showing off their bravery?

PEER PRESSURE

Are you under a lot of peer pressure
To do things that you feel aren't right?
The fear of being rejected among the group
Puts you into a terrible plight.
What should you do in this predicament?
Well, it's much easier than you think.
Friends that are really worth keeping
Won't con you, to make your values shrink.
Speak up when you feel something is wrong,
Don't just go along with the crowd.
Be the good example for others to follow
And they will make you proud.

BREAKING UP

Breaking up with your sweetheart
And you're really down in the dumps.
Such a loss is devastating;
It hurts and you're feeling the lumps.
Couples never agree on everything,
But love can help make proper decisions.
If either or both are too selfish
It's tough to make any revisions.
You should want the best for your sweetheart,
And the same feelings returned to you.
Either compromise or sacrifice
When you know it's the right thing to do.
You must have trust in each other,
And feelings of jealousy won't work.
Trust is a must or something will bust,
And untrue thoughts and words really hurt.
When building a lasting relationship
Couples should work out plans together.
Building their love on a solid foundation
So it can withstand - "Whatever."
The most solid foundation to build on
Is faith in the Lord Jesus Christ.
With Him all things are possible,
On Him build your husband or wife.

GROWN-UP KIDS

You may not feel like a kid at your age,
But to Mom or Dad you're their child.
They have your best interest at heart,
Even when they're driving you wild.
I'm going to take the parents side here
Because I have grown-up kids too.
I have some thoughts on the subject
That could be relevant to you.
We have all seen how teenagers think,
They seem sure that "they know it all."
If you're in your thirties or forties now,
With some thought, you may recall?
Loving parents with teenage kids
May often be put to the test.
And despite what those "know it alls" know,
They'll attempt to guide them their best.
Experience is a really good teacher,
And most parents learn the hard way.
They could avoid you some hardships too,
If you adhere to what they say.
I wish that I had been smart enough
To use my parents' advice as a mold.
Life would be much easier on me
If I had fed on what I was told.
I grow older and wiser each day,
Realizing I'm not as bright as I thought.
And if I hadn't been one "know it all" son,
My life would be far better wrought.
The same goes now as when you were a teen,
This isn't meant to make your confidence shrink.
And even though - "you're sure that you know,"
You may not be as smart as you think.

BLAME SOMEONE ELSE?

I can't understand why I did this;
I'm so ashamed of myself.
And there's no way to justify it.
Should I blame somebody else?
Screw-ups happen to all of us,
But we learn from our mistakes.
Blaming someone else to cover yourself
Is utterly ruthless and only for snakes.
Even if you get by with it,
Framing another to carry your shame,
You'll lose much pride, knowing inside,
You've caused another to bear your pain.
What if you don't get by with it
And the actual truth comes out?
Then all will know what a viper you are
And you'll lose more than your clout.
Show some backbone - own up to it;
This builds character and grows respect.
Mistakes are usually good teachers,
And you've made one - what the heck?
Chalk up lessons learned the hard way.
Never allow your honor or stature to shrink.
Admit blunders you shouldn't have made,
The outcome is seldom as bad as you think.

WORRYING

Are you a perpetual "worry wart,"
Constantly fearing the worst,
Afraid that something will happen
To cause your bubble to burst?
I once fit into this category,
A jittery bundle of nerves
Worrying about family and friends
As life would throw us some curves.
My sister gave me some good advice,
Passed down to her from Dad
As he pulled her close with a soothing hug
When she was worried so bad.
Wiping the tears from her eyes he said,
"There's nothing to be worrying about.
If you can't correct whatever's going on,
It'll just have to work itself out."
"Don't be fearing and fretting so,
'May baby' this isn't the answer.
Worrying doesn't help the least little bit,
But it'll eat you up like a cancer."
I don't worry about anything anymore,
I just take it all in as it comes.
I may get mad as hell and cuss and yell
And pound on my war drums.
This way I get it out of my system,
Then it's completely over and done.
I try to be "happy go lucky,"
Get ornery, and have some fun.
I hope you use this to settle your stress,
Relinquishing the worrying attitude.
Then you can give me a pat on the back, -
To Sis I must show my gratitude.

NEEDING ADVICE

I'm asking for advice on this one;
I've heard about it all my life.
Didn't give it much thought before,
But now, it's me and my wife.
I've loved "my sweetheart" from the start
And have grown to love her more o'er the years.
But now she thinks that I don't understand her
And will start griping and end up in tears.
I should be easier to live with now,
Having learned from many mistakes.
She's "the most important part of my life,"
What's happening? - For goodness sakes!
I try to treat her the best I know how,
Maybe expecting a bit more than a thank you.
But lately she'll yell and scream and get real mean,
And can manage to get quite rank, too.
Has a demon taken possession of her?
If it's hormones - how long does it last?
Many of you have experienced this.
Will she return to normal after it's passed?
I'm trying to understand the thinking here -
Calling this change of life - menopause.
Is it because men get under their skin?
Is there some way to mend the cause?

RESPONSE TO NEEDING ADVICE

There are two sides to every argument;
This is in response to your "Needing Advice."
I'm currently going through menopause now
And I feel sorry for that jackass's wife.
Most of the time I'm feeling hard as ice
And nothing can be done to melt it.
I know that I'm wrong when I get to carrying on,
But the truth - I simply can't help it.
To answer those ignorant questions of his:
There's no "damned demon" inside.
Menopause has been around forever, you jerk,
What's happened? - Has your brain died?
You "butt hole," we're not carbon copies,
No one knows how long it will last.
It's tougher on some more than others,
And we all hope that soon it will pass.
We realize we're hard to live with,
And we know when we go to excess.
It's not that we don't still love you,
But right now it's too hard to express.
My advice to you is, "keep your big mouth shut."
I do understand your concern.
That "lovely lady" is still in there somewhere,
Be patient and she will return.

TO PARENTS TODAY

My brother is six years older than I
And he has a very high I.Q.
Over the years he has taught me many things,
One of which I will share now with you.
He taught me to mind my parents
And never give them any lip.
He unknowingly taught me this
At the cost of hurtin' his hip.
I don't know what my brother did,
And I don't know what he said.
But he got a slap and then the razor strap,
And was sent straight up to bed.
I wasn't told anything about it.
What happened was never mentioned.
But what I saw when I was small
Sure brought me to attention.
When I was told to do somethin',
They didn't have to repeat.
I knew they meant just what they said,
And I didn't wanna get beat.
My parent didn't really have to beat us
Because they spanked us when we were young.
We were taught to respect our elders
And to be careful with our tongue.
To parents today - what can I say?
You're told that spanking shouldn't be used.
If you give them the belt and make sure that it's felt,
You might be charged with child abuse.
Kids anymore show no respect,
Especially for Mom and Dad.
Teachers are low on the totem pole
And preachers almost as bad.

You might send your kids to a Catholic school,
Those nuns teach respect, at least.
But accordin' to the news media,
Don't let 'em alone with a priest!
I recommend that you don't be their friend.
They must look up to you.
You should rule and guide, and yes "tan their hides."
Make sure they do what they're told to do.
You have got to be consistent
And punish them good when they are little.
For goodness sake, they're not gonna break;
Youngsters are not very brittle.
Don't misunderstand what I'm saying,
Don't injure the little squirt.
But punishment should be punishment.
It has darn sure gotta hurt!
Yes, spanking is the way to go,
You don't wanna end up with a brat.
Like my brother taught me, let the other kids see,
And know they don't want nonna that.

MOTHER AND SON

I took my mother for granted,
Assuming she'd always be there for me.
Even when she said, "I'm getting so tired,"
I wasn't listening adequately.
She was trying to tell me that she would be leaving
To her "heavenly home up above."
I wasn't willing to accept the thought of losing her
And being without her motherly love.
I should have been paying better attention,
Should have hugged her more when she was near.
She was always there to give loving care
When help was needed, she was so dear.
I wish I'd tried to do more for her,
She made feel like I was "number one."
This may not be fact but she had the knack
For special feelings from mother to son.
Are you fortunate enough to still have Mom?
If so, please learn from my mistakes.
Show her often how much she means to you
And help her, for goodness sakes.
Give her some loving care when she needs it
And do something that I should have done.
Tell her that she's the "number one" mother
And you're so proud to be her son.

FAMILY, FRIENDS, AND FEELINGS

LIFE ZIPS BY

The older I get the more I realize
How veritably short life is.
Here today and gone tomorrow.
Our lives zip by in a whiz.
What can we do to make the best of it?
Of the short time we have left?
For me Sweetheart, when I'm with you
Is the time that I love best.

With love always

WHO'S WHO

Who's Who in America,
The publication that tells us who's who.
I couldn't find your name listed,
And MY most important who is "You."

SWEETEST DAY

It's the third Saturday in October,
But we can change that in the neatest way.
Whenever we're together, dear,
Will be our "Sweetest Day."

Tom

SPECIAL THINGS

How pretty are the redbud trees
When they blossom out in Spring,
The sun above is shining bright
And the songbirds, how they sing.
The multitude of wildflowers,
Their pleasant odors fill the air.
The honeybees are busy
Gathering nectar everywhere.
I sit beneath this big oak tree
And watch the sparkling of the dew,
When I realize all these special things
Are found when I'm with you.
The redbud with its heart shaped leaves,
Saying, "Would you be my Valentine?"
Whenever you are with me
The sun will always shine.
I hear the songbirds singing
When I pull you close to me.
To smell the wildflowers in your hair
Is such a luxury.
And Oh! The sweet nectar of your lips;
I must keep the bees away.
And the sparkle in your eyes
Is brighter than the dew on any day.
I don't know how to say it,
To express your many charms,
But storm clouds turn to sunshine
When you are in my arms.
I sit beneath this big oak tree;
How I wish you were here with me.

SUE

You've been my sweetheart for quite a spell;
I won't embarrass you by mentioning the years.
We have shared most of our lives together, dear:
Good times, heartaches and tears.
I know I leave a lot to be desired, sometimes;
We both can get on each other's nerves.
But we've always been able to work things out,
Even when life throws us some curves.
We were meant for each other from day one;
At first sight, I fell in love with you.
Then when we kissed, your lips on mine
Told me that you loved me, too.
Now our health appears to be going downhill,
Life gives us both clouds and sunshine.
Sweetheart, I've always loved you and I always will,
You'll always be my Valentine.

Happy Valentine's Day!

TO SIS FROM TOM

Was gonna write you a letter,
Didn't know what to say,
So I'll just send you some of my poems
And let you know I'm OK.
Hope my English teacher
Never gets to readin' these;
She'd mark 'em up with red and blue;
I'd be lucky to get D's.
Tell Gail and Janie I say, "Hello."
Hope they're doin' well.
I want to make it out there someday,
But only time will tell.
You've told me how proud you are of Brooke,
I'm sure she's a sweet young lady.
Kids grow up so fast you know,
Oh yes, and "how's the baby?"
I guess I'd better go for now,
It's a shame we're so far apart.
I just wanted to let you know,
You're <u>always</u> in my heart.

TO NANCY

I know you haven't heard from me,
But I've been thinking much of you.
You've suffered such a terrible loss
And I wish there was something I could do.
I've started to call you several times,
Then wondering: what would I say?
If I could have said something I thought would help,
I'd have called you right away.
I know that when I speak with you
We might both end up in tears.
I guess I always chicken out,
Afraid to face my fears.
I'm ashamed of myself for going so long
Without you hearing from me.
I apologize. I am so sorry.
That's no way to treat family.
If there's anything I can do for you,
I've done so little in the past;
I want you to know right here and now,
All you have to do is ask.

Love,
Tom

SWEETHEART

You wished me a Happy Valentine's Day
And you gave me a big hug and kiss.
And I told you that I was broke
And wouldn't be giving you a gift.
You said, "Don't worry about that.
You just have a very nice day."
And you gave me another hug and kiss,
Saying, "Things will work out OK."
Well, I'm broke but I have a pencil
And I can come up with a rhyme.
"I'll love my wife for the rest of my life
Because you are my Valentine."

TO SUZI

Suzi, you have so much on your mind
That you can't get a good night's sleep.
I have been there before myself, for sure,
And counted many a sheep.
Sometimes when a loved one is taken away
We feel that we are to blame.
We think that God doesn't spare the rod
And we are being punished for our shame.
I no longer believe this to be the case,
I don't think He works this way.
I do believe He will punish us all,
But not until judgment day.
Theresa lost her only child,
Her healthy twenty year old son.
If she was being punished,
What in the world could she have done?
You keep thinking about the unborn child
That was taken away from you.
You wonder why it was taken away,
But there was nothing you could do.
God's mighty plan we can't understand,
We just accept that He knows best.
So tonight when you lay your pretty head down,
Ease your mind and please get some rest.

THE GATHERING PLACE

I stop nearly every morning
At the little country Gathering Place,
The food is great, the service is good,
But it's the people that give it taste.
I like to get there early,
Just as they open up,
And smell the coffee a brewin'
And maybe get first cup.
Randy will stand up on a chair
And wiggle the fluorescent light.
It's kinda like me, it don't wanna wake up,
But soon it's burning bright.
Suzi will greet me with a smile
And have something neat to say.
She has a way of making me feel real good;
Sure brightens up my day.
The regulars come in one at a time.
They'll nod or say hello.
Ron reads the Wall Street Journal,
Wayne gets coffee to go.
Richard will sit and talk to me,
He keeps me well informed.
Bob drives up in his big ol' truck
And Ledger taps his horn.
Someone will get something started
And offer a point of view.
No one seems to be bashful,
So you hear the other sides, too.
Oh no! It's seven-thirty,
It's time for me to go.
Here comes Theresa, she'll keep things going
For the next half hour or so.

THE CLOUD

Linda, our waitress, asked us,
"Which one of you guys up and died?"
Richard said, "It wasn't me."
But I was a thinkin' he'd lied.
Everyone's a checkin' each other out
To see who might be a blushin'.
But nobody will give themselves away,
Dead quiet from everyone hushin'.
I finally said, "Whoever did that,
Stand up and take a bow!
There's never been an odor like this before,
We should notify Guinness right now."
Mike, in the kitchen, opened the back door
And stuck his head out in the breeze.
That floated another cloud into the dining room;
Then we knew who was cuttin' the cheese.

MR. FIX-IT

I asked Richard to fix my truck,
He can do most anything.
But the best thing about him doin' the job,
Is a listenin' to him explain:
"The wicker-bill sets on the hypucker-por-arm,
Just behind the stationary smoke shifter.
The triple-stringer, suspended from a sky hook,
Was used to jack it off the lifter."
"After I got that out of the way,
I needed a left-handed monkey wrench
To take out the wobble-shaft,
And set it on the bench."
"With the cram-crusher, I made some pigeon milk,
To loosen up the thing-ah-ma-bob in the kranny.
That stuff ag-u-lates the pracilla-pods,
Like a puttin' alka-seltzer in brandy."
"I've tried to make this plain and simple,
And you were really lucky.
I was able to fix it with my dume-ah-flidget
Using goop and uck-um-pucky."

DESARAE

So this is your twentieth birthday.
Those childhood years have all gone by.
The years as a youngster seem to drag on,
But watch now how time will fly.
It's easy to see that you have grown up,
Especially this past year.
I've watched a little teenage punk
Turn into a lady who's sweet and dear.
Like your mother and Mike, I'm proud of you,
And wish you all of the best.
Life is full of many different challenges,
But I'm sure you can stand the test.
You've got your life on track right now,
And you're getting back in school.
Cosmetology sounds like a promising career,
But please practice on some other fool.
I was too cheap to buy you a card,
So I wrote you these lines, Desarae.
Again I wish you ALL OF THE BEST!
And have a very Happy Birthday!

OL' PAUL LORENTZ

One of my friends, ol' Paul Lorentz,
Has true rhythm with his guitar.
But there's a couple of things that hold him back
Or he could be a "Big Star."
The first sad thing is he just can't sing,
But he sure can strum and peck.
He'll pick and pang to get that perfect "twang"
That'll send chills down the back of your neck.
I've never seen fingers move like his
To create the genuine pitch.
And he'll change a cord or tone so fast
You'd think a magician had made the switch.
He can dream up new tunes and play so well,
He oughtta be able to sell some.
But the other thing that definitely holds him back, -
He's even uglier than Willie Nelson!

HOW MANY?

I couldn't help overhearing
As Bill was questioning Joe.
"I'm cooking dinner for our Inspection,
How many brethren do think will show?"
Joe attends all the Inspections,
So he should be the one to ask.
But getting a helpful answer from him,
Was definitely quite a task.
He said, "There were several at Goshen,
And quite a few at Aberdeen,
Not so many at Owensville,
And Amelia was pretty lean."
"Williamsburg had a breakfast,
A whole bunch showed up over there.
I've learned to follow Herman around,
He's first in line everywhere."
"Ripley was really crowded,
And Marathon was full to the brim.
No big deal at Loveland,
And Bethel was pretty slim."
Bill said, "Pardon me, Joe, for interrupting you,
I know you weren't quite finished yet.
But, I'm, asking YOU, our Education Officer,
How many plates do you think I should set?"

THE FAMOUS PAUL BACK

Paul Back is an artist in woodworking;
He's a master when it comes to the finish.
He'll sand, stain, and polyurethane,
And when he's done, there'll be no blemish.
He can create wonders with all kinds of wood.
His craft has endorsed him much fame.
He is now well known far and wide
From Edenton to Pleasant Pain.
He doesn't like to take all the credit,
He makes that perfectly clear.
He acknowledges his friend, Orville Ramsey,
As the actual "design engineer."
But Jerry Ross set me straight
When he said, "This ain't just a hunch.
I've known both of those jokers for quite a spell
And their wives are the brains of the bunch."

RAY MOON
AND TABLE ETIQUETTE

Ray Moon is somethin' to behold when he's eatin',
He never uses napkins or bibs.
I wish Gloria Vanderbilt or Martha Stewart
Could watch him eatin' barbecued ribs.
He'd be a wearin' his bib overalls
And a tee shirt without any sleeves,
So the grease can run down to his elbows
Before it drips onto his knees.
He's not too bad with the first slab,
But he's awesome with the next two batches.
You might compare him a tanglin' with those ribs
To Big Time Wrestlin' matches.
I believe Gloria or Martha would gasp and faint,
Then write a full book about Ray.
I asked him his thoughts on pompous criticism,
And here's what he had to say:
"They try to tell me what fork to use,
But I don't need any fork,
Eatin' ribs wasn't meant to be pretty,
It's an actual contact sport."

AN HONEST LEADER

We were blessed by having good parents
And growing up on a small farm.
We would work and play during the day
And sleep at night, fearing no harm.
Dad was a school board member,
And he was a township trustee;
He was also a deacon in our church,
A true leader in our community.
Mom could out-work any two men,
She was in a class of her own.
Her title was housewife and mother,
And we were mothered even after we'd grown.
She fixed three good meals every day
That we enjoyed at the table together.
Chatting at meals was commonplace,
And the more conversation, the better.
We could all voice our very own thoughts;
With so many opinions, what should we do?
With Dad at the head of the table,
His decisions would stick like glue.
I wish our country could run as well,
With elected officials stating what they feel is best;
And having an honest leader making the final say,
Putting all of our minds at rest.
We always respected Dad's decisions,
For we knew he would do what was right.
If we could trust our leaders as I did my parents,
We would all sleep better at night.

THE BIG COON HUNT

Jim Lambert and I decided to go
To the championship hunt of the P.K.C.
The top hunters and hounds from all fifty states;
We thought that'd be somethin' to see.
I didn't expect to win anythin' -
I just wanted to check it out,
And meet some of those big name breeders and dogs
That I'd been a readin' about.
Jim, on the other hand, had a good hound
That he thought might even place.
But our main goal was to just have a good time
And meet the big shots face to face.
When we got there and put up the fee,
We were divided into casts of four.
Points were given for first strike and first tree,
And minus for wrong or poor.
Jim and I were in different casts.
I was with Duell Eads, Charlie Moon and Joe Barr.
I had heard of these notorious names before;
Jim hunted with a Richardson, Wilson and Carr.
Barr's cur bitch, "Daisy", seemed kinda lazy,
Didn't wanna get out of the truck.
And when turned loose, she cornered a goose,
"Joe, Sorry 'bout your luck."
Moon's red-bone, "Prime Rib", was a babblin' dog,
All he did was babbler and boo.
But Mooney continually bragged him up
And was a tryin' to sell him, too.
My plot, "Jack" was a leadin' the pack,
First to strike and first to tree.
But when we got there, a grin and stare
Of a possum was all we could see.

Duell's English, "Duke", won by a fluke;
He was old and slow at best.
But he finally struck and treed a coon, indeed,
And won our cast by no contest.
Jim's black and tan he called "Big Man"
Found a still, and heck - he got drunk.
Richardson's walker dog, "Hank," smellin' quite rank
Came back a draggin' a skunk.
Wilson's blue tick, "Old Blue," got sick.
He kept a rubbin' his butt on the ground.
He either had worms or some other germs;
I think he'll get sent to pound.
Carr's mutt, "Cooner," he was a sooner, -
Sooner eat than anythin' else.
He'd just follow old Fred and Jim finally said,
"You might as well hunt by yourself."
Jim's cast with no points, some a smokin' their joints
As they drove back to the clubhouse, disgusted.
They were all drinkin' beer and that's when we hear
How the favorites to win got busted.
The Brown boys were kin and nearly always would win,
They're the biggest name breeders - no doubt!
But a new judge named Long figured somethin' was wrong,
And he was gonna straighten it out.
The Browns walker hounds had outstanding scores
But Long knew they'd either cheat or fudge.
So he had them watched close and gave them a dose,
Both were scratched by this true, honest judge.
Then while a drivin' back home - relivin' the night,
We ended up a feelin' so dumb.
We drove so far for this gigantic hunt
And neither of us knew who had won.

LOOKIN' GOOD

When Bill Jones visits the nursing homes,
He'll look around and say, "You're lookin' good."
Then he'll play and sing and entertain,
And dance a little more than he should.
He'll pick his itty-bitty banjo,
That he's had since he was a child.
But what impresses me is his ability,
To sing - and his humor and dress are wild.
He wears black pants with black suspenders,
And a pumpkin orange shirt that I shouldn't knock,
And he'll start his dance and raise up his pants
To show one red and one blue sock.
Between tunes he'll tell funny stories.
Some will laugh while others might grin.
When he gets the chance, he'll again raise his pants,
And say, "I've another pair at home just like 'em."
When I greeted him this morning,
What I said bugged him more than it should.
His expression changed and his jaw dropped
When I said, "Bill - you're lookin' good."

THE BIG SHRIMP RUN

Jerry Ross, Orville Ramsey and Paul Back
    Spend the winter in Florida each year.
They had planned a short trip early this fall
    Because the big shrimp run was near.
Their winter neighbors had told them about it,
    And they were gonna be ready and set.
None of 'em had ever done it before,
    But were willin' to get their feet wet.
    These guys are all big eaters
And free shrimp sounded dog-gone good.
And if their moron friend was a catchin' 'em,
    They knew darn well that they could.
    Then Orville's back went out of whack
And Paul and Jerry went south without him,
    Promisin' to bring back coolers of shrimp,
    Tellin' Orville not to worry about 'em.
    Upon their arrival Jerry said to Paul:
    "I'll only need to see it done once,
    Then I'll know as much as a pro,
    I'll prove to you I'm no dunce."
So Jerry tagged along with the neighbor,
Who threw his net, and with one tug and pull
    Drew it up against the boat
    And had shrimp by the bucketsful.
    So Jerry took Paul that afternoon
    To show him just how it was done.
    But Jerry with his new motor boat
    Couldn't find any shrimp run.

They tossed their net for hours
And were gonna head back to shore
When the boat motor ran out of gas
And their total shrimp count was four.
Jerry quickly said, "I'm the Captain,
It's my duty to stay here with my boat.
You'll have to go get us some fuel,
When you get tired of swimmin', just float."
While they're fussin', another boat came along
That had some extra fuel mix.
But neither of these tight-wads paid for the gas
That got them out of their fix.
They no more than got back from their adventure
When Orville phoned, and his mouth was a waterin'.
He couldn't wait to hear the details
Of his buddies massive shrimp slaughterin'.
Paul answered the phone and told a big fib
Of their catch bein' hijacked by some mobster.
But he promised that Jerry would pick up the tab
When they all went out to Red Lobster.

BROKEN FAMILY

Just want everyone to know
My feelings haven't changed.
I still love you all so very much,
Even with the family estranged.
I've missed some graduations,
Missed some weddings, too.
I have a niece I've never seen
And that really makes me blue.
I miss your smiling faces
And the fun we used to have.
We used to get together
Just to make each other laugh.
Now Mom and Dad have left this world,
I guess they held the key.
I pray to God that He might mend
This broken family.

SWEET DREAMS

I walk along this narrow path
With the full moon up above.
The air is clear and pleasant,
Perfect for those in love.
The sky is so blue with its brightness,
I might even think it was day.
But I see the stars, how they twinkle
In such a magical way.
All at once a falling star
Flashes across the sky!
I make a wish that I know won't come true,
While asking myself, "Why?"
I wish that you were here with me,
You know I belong to you.
Sitting down by this peaceful brook
I wonder what to do.
Gazing into the rippling water
And what do you think I see?
A reflection of us together, dear,
Making love so passionately.
But I awake and walk back the path,
Still with the beautiful skies,
Thinking of my wonderful dream,
Now with tears in my eyes.
It seems I spend my life dreaming,
Yes, dreaming and thinking of you.
If we could only be together again
And make these dreams come true.
It's wrong to have such a perfect night,
Full moon with a lovely glowing tone,
Twinkling stars and this peaceful brook,
And to walk this path alone.

GOOD STORY-TELLIN'

Good story tellin' takes some practice.
Webster defines it as an art.
You must keep your audience's attention,
And make it interestin', right from the start.
When depictin' particular characters
You've got to act and sound like them.
That paints a picture of authenticity,
But you'll add a little vigor and vim.
Now when a tellin' this true story,
Don't follow it right to the letter.
Use your vivid imagination,
And make that true story better.
I have a friend, who's exceptionally good;
His voice is deep and crisp.
He'll keep you on the edge of your seat,
With him, it's a natural gift.
He's a brilliant public speaker,
And with his good humor and wit
He can make the dullest theme enjoyable,
By stretchin' the truth a bit.
And he can mimic almost anyone;
He'll copy 'em head to toe.
And when he spits his T-backer into that cup,
You can expect a real show.
The only complaint you'll ever hear
Is when he gets his chrome dome right under the light.
The glare and the shine will make you go blind
And to miss any of his mimic ain't right.
I could go on and on about him,
But I'll stop, without a lot more said.
The best story-teller I've ever known
Is my good friend "Moose", Bob Moorhead.

ORVILLE RAMSEY – THIS IS YOUR LIFE

I was asked to write this for your party.
The request came from your dear wife.
So she alone is the one to blame;
Orville Ramsey, "This Is Your Life."
Born on October nineteenth,
Nineteen and Thirty-Seven,
To Pearl and Samuel Ramsey
You were a precious little gift from Heaven.
As a child, you would pick your own corner
Where you felt safe, without any fear,
And you would sit there and make your own jewelry.
Good practice for a "design engineer."
You grew up in downtown Cincinnati
Where you met some pretty neat guys,
Who taught you some of the facts of life
That made you real street wise.
Like when you were just about seven
Your new shoes were ripped-off by neighborhood bros.
You learned not to be a travelin' alone
When a wearin' any new clothes.
Your teenage years they taught you some more
When you worked odd jobs for nickels and dimes.
Gettin' home with the money was the hard part,
You were ice-picked a couple of times.
Startin' at the bottom with Leugers Furniture,
This is how the story goes:
You advanced quickly from upholsterer to manager
With little skill and lots of brown nose.
I understand you were quite the "ladies man,"
But you were never one to boast
When I asked if you had ever been married before
Your answer was: "Yes, more than most.
But Debbie, my sweetheart, my own dear love
Is the truest and best part of my life.
And if she will continue to tolerate me,
We'll always be husband and wife."

79

You have always liked huntin' and fishin',
And boatin' and campin', too.
You loved to take the kids on campin' trips.
Luckily no one drowned when you tipped the canoe.
I've heard that you're good with children;
When you're around, they always seem glad.
Rumor has it that everyone's kids
Want to call you "Granddad."
You were really proud of your only deer.
You bagged it with a compound bow.
Then tied it to the top of your station wagon
To put on a real big show.
You drove to Clermont North Eastern School
Where Debbie's job was to keep the kids in line.
You parked up against the school building
And the kids had a really good time.
The principal asked Debbie who the clown was
With the deer and puttin' on a show.
She, bein' the honest person she is,
Said, "Sir, I swear I don't know!"
Now that retirement has come around
You can goof off with your buddies.
I've been a checkin' these friends of yours out
And none are old fuddy-duddies.
Well, this is your birthday party
And Martin asked, "What should we do for a gift?"
I said, "Nothin', our attendin' the party should be enough."
But he thought that wasn't too swift.
He said that Home Depot is your favorite place,
A gift certificate from there, for sure.
But when we got to countin' our money,
We went with the Dollar Store.
Samuel Clements rode in on the comet,
Orville Ramsey drifted in after the flood.
Orville, everyone here is proud to be your good friend.
HAPPY BIRTHDAY, BUD!

BILL MILLER'S T-BUCKET

Bill Miller is a pillar of the T-Bucket clan,
He's the president of his group.
For those who still don't know about Bill,
I've been asked to give you the scoop.
He has never met a stranger,
Not at all shy, with a great gift of gab.
He wears a beard, pony-tail and bib overalls
To cover some ugly and flab.
When you first see Bill you might think
That he has a growth on his jaw.
But in a little bit, he'll have to spit,
Then you know that the lump is his "chaw."
Hot Wheel cars, "T-Buckets", is his prime time now,
And it's here that he has most of this fun.
I would like to wish Bill and Tom Gish
Good luck, for they're both out to be number one.
It was Tom that asked me to write this,
I must give credit where credit is due.
He is my sole source of information,
And I assume what he told me is true.
Bill is now about to go all out.
Because he hasn't fared well in the past.
Last year in Kentucky, accordin' to Tom,
He actually came in dead last.
When he saw the numerous entries in the Hot Wheel line,
He put his T-Bucket in a different bracket.
This way he had only two others to beat.
And thought he'd have a better whack at it.
Realizin' Bill's entry was in the wrong group
Was the judge's determining factor.
So Bill wasn't too lucky in Kentucky;
The winner was a John Deere tractor.

Bill is gearin' up for his third national show,
He's bought a second bucket to work on his first.
He also invested ten grand on a blower.
He intends to put an end to his bad luck curse.
When I asked him his fate in the Briar State,
He didn't know that I'd already heard.
He told me straight up, "I didn't win -
But you know, I did come in third."

BRYAN AND JEAN'S HONEYMOON

Bryan Lewis married Jean Elam
When she was young and in full bloom,
And they hurriedly drove to Gatlinburg,
To spend their honeymoon.
Just as they entered Gatlinburg
He slipped his hand between her knees.
Jean whispered gently in his ear,
"We're married, you can go further, please."
Humorously obedient to her request,
As she rubbed on his bazooka,
Bryan pulled his hand away,
And drove on to Chattanooga.
There he wanted to play Pony Express.
"What's that?" she asked, in dainty nightgown.
"It's kinda like Spin the Bottle," he said,
"But a little more horsin' around."
After days and nights of continual horseplay,
Bryan got tired and faked having the flu.
Jean rushed him to a local doctor
For advice on what to do.
He told her, "Your husband doesn't look very well,
He needs rest and should sleep like a log."
She said, "Doc, I know that he's ugly,
But he's good to me and the dog."
"He's fairly attractive when I keep the lights dim,
And that's when I love him the best."
"Can you fix him up, Doc? He's so well endowed,
And he's awesome at Pony Express!"

THE GOLDEN ANNIVERSARY OF NEAL AND SADIE BROWN

Belinda asked me to come up with a rhyme
To read at your Golden Anniversary celebration.
She later hit me with some restrictions
Endorsed by her sibling delegation.
"You must NOT embarrass anyone,
And keep it short and sweet."
Heck! That's like tryin' to fix a good meal
With no potatoes or meat.
I could ask my truck to last forever,
But you don't get any oil or grease,
Or tell my junk-yard dog to guard the place,
Then pull out all his teeth.
But here goes - I'm gonna try it,
Because you deserve our congratulations:
Sadie and Neal, your love must be real,
And you're darn good at human relations.
I have some good stories to tell on Neal
That most of you would think are neat,
But I will fulfill my promise
And keep it nice and short and sweet.
So Neal and Sadie I'll stop right here
By wishing you a very happy Golden Anniversary.
And I hope we'll be able to do this again
To honor - your Diamond Jubilee.

MY NAMESAKE

I'm so proud of you, young Thomas.
Your mother named you after me.
She's my only daughter;
A very special luxury.
We must keep a secret from her, though.
Don't ever tell your mommy.
When we're together, man to man,
I'm gonna call you Tommy.

RAY'S HOSPITAL STAY

I don't know how to put this,
I should just keep my big mouth shut.
But I will spew as I always do,
And get myself into a rut.
You think that I'm a pretty good guy
Because I've been coming to see you.
When this is shown and the truth is known
You'll look at me and say P.U.
Ray, I hope you don't get real mad
And poke me in the kisser.
You're the patient in the hospital,
But I've been coming to see your sister.

JUST THINK

Ray, we're alone in your rehab home,
Just think of this combination.
Neither of us hear and you can't talk,
What an interesting conversation.

THE TRUTH HURTS

I asked my sweetheart to level with me,
"Tell me the truth and I'll understand."
Well, she did and hit me with a low blow,
Saying she has another man.
"I guess he's tall, dark and handsome,"
I say angrily, and listen to her speak true.
"No, he's really short and chubby,
But not nearly as fat as you!"

BILL AND JUNE MARTIN'S GOLDEN WEDDING ANNIVERSARY

When June Terwilliger met Bill Martin
She wasn't at all impressed.
But when Bill saw her his brain went astir
And his whole body was mighty distressed.
She was just right, it was love at first sight,
But somehow June didn't know it.
But Bill, he knew that his love was true,
And he'd do whatever it took to show it.
Didn't have any phone - couldn't leave her alone,
Devised uncanny reasons to stop over.
But the Terwilligers had many a flesh eatin' guinea
That actually ate the neighbor's dog, Rover.
Right from the start Bill was a brave heart,
No birds could keep him away.
They gave him no slack with their vicious attack,
But he'd fight his way in, anyway.
Then June realized he was makin' up lies
Just to be over there with her.
That little spark lit the fire in her heart
As he finally got nerve enough to kiss her.
Bill made a mistake on their first real date
When he took her to his favorite saloon.
It was his plan to be the real "he man,"
But this didn't set well with June.
To make a long story short, bein' a good sport,
She walked herself home through the woods.
She proved her point to Bill and his joint
That she could take care of herself and her goods.
As their love grew and June knew it was true
There was lots of huggin' and kissin',
Then Bill made bigger plans for roving hands
A wonderin' what he'd been a missin'.

As they were a parkin' and heavily sparkin'
There wasn't much room in the Volkswagon Beetle.
But right from the go, June abruptly said, "No!"
"Not 'til we're married and legal."
They put their wedding plans in the preacher's hands
And were married right in his house.
And when they said, "I do" - they meant it too,
Not a spittin' just words from their mouths.
They rented a place in old Milford;
Didn't splurge on a big honeymoon.
The place wasn't much but it worked in a clutch
For the needs of the new bride and groom.
Later they moved to Newtonsville - then again to Price Hill.
I don't know for sure if this is true;
But rumor has it from a reliable source,
They would move as the rent came due.
Then the kids came along and you can't do kids wrong;
Must see that the young uns grow up real good.
So for the kids and for fun - moved back to Edenton, -
Their grass roots neighborhood.
Vicky told me when Billy and she were little,
They'd hear their Dad sing while swingin' his palm:
"June Bug, June Bug sittin' on a really rock"
And they knew he was singin' 'bout Mom.
Then Vicky said, "That don't make any sense,
I must be rememberin' it wrong."
I said, "No, Bill has always been a meatcutter.
He probably just butchered the song."
I can hear in my mind Bill a singin':
"June Bug, June Bug let's try out the new rug,"
And I can see June give him the evil eye,
Then sing, "Bill-et, Bill-et want hit with this skillet?"
That would be June's reply.

Well I hope my teasin' isn't too displeasin',
I never know what'll come out of my pen.
Blame Vicky - she asked me to write this,
And I did, 'cause I am your friend.
I would like to render a special thanks
To Vicky and Billy, our hosts.
Bill and June, I will end this soon,
But there's a little more here for you both.
This is your Golden Anniversary!
A marriage of fifty years.
You've hung in there together no matter what;
Through good times, hard times and tears.
You've raised a very close knit family
Who think the world of you.
You've always been pillars of this community.
Everyone here is so proud of you two.
Your marriage is an example for us to follow;
All couples have troubles somewhere.
You've proven that problems can be worked out;
We know that you've had your share.
Congratulations, Mr. and Mrs. Martin,
Happy Golden Anniversary!
And I hope we can all get together again
For your Diamond Jubilee.

FROM MOM TO YOU

A mother's love is so special.
It's in a class of its own.
Her love for you is strong and true,
Even when not always shown.
I'm writing this for your mom
To send to you in Iraq.
When I asked her, "What should I say?"
She seemed to fall off track.
Was she conveniently speechless?
No - words couldn't pass through her throat.
Not that she didn't want to say something.
She was unable to make a quote.
Using her feelings that emitted in silence
This poem I was able to start.
I easily knew the fear of losing you
Was eating away at her heart.
I feel she may not have told you enough,
But she really loves you a lot.
And a mother's love is a gift from above.
And she'll love you - no matter what!

FAYE

Faye, you are the mother of five.
You should be so proud.
You are now the head of this family tree,
Whose number makes quite a crowd.
You are for sure the main feature
For all of us to gather around.
When you're the center of attention,
The love just seems to abound.
A "mothers love" seems to flow about
And falls on everyone.
And the older she grows the more her love flows,
And shines on us all like the sun.
There are lots of mothers in this group,
But you are the head of the bunch.
So just let yourself take it easy today,
And allow us take you to lunch.
It's kind of absurd to try to find words,
For all the love here for you, Faye.
It was a request from Sue that I write this for you,
From all of us - Happy Mothers Day!

HAPPY MOTHER'S DAY

I like to write a little more lately
To those on my "sweet and dear" list.
I should have written and read this to you
When you were still here to hear this.
When I told you back then that "I love you,"
Somehow I didn't realize how much.
"Motherly Love" is continual, lasting forever;
Sometimes I still need your loving touch.
You left here to see Dad some time ago,
To join him in that "heavenly place."
But you still manage to help when I need you;
In my dreams we speak face to face.
Mom, I'm getting some tears in my eyes right now,
I must be feeling sorry for myself.
I just wanted to say "Happy Mother's Day;
Your motherly love is true wealth."

"With love more than ever" - - - Tom

TO LORI – FROM MOM

You've graduated from high school
And Mom is so proud of you.
A major hurdle has been cleared.
Now what do you plan to do?
You're not a child any longer,
You've grown up, for goodness sakes.
You'll be making some big decisions now;
Always learn from your mistakes.
Yes, even you will make some,
Why? - Because all of us do.
Sometimes we listen to poor advice
And ignore good advice, too.
Even being mature we can't always be sure,
We just up and go with our hunches.
And when a decision turns out to be wrong
We must learn to roll with the punches.
Obviously, you and Mom are very close
And think the world of each other.
And when you do make a major mistake
Feel free to discuss it with Mother.
She will continue to have your best interest at heart,
Even now that you are grown.
And "no matter what," she'll understand,
Because Mom has made mistakes of her own.
Well so much for that,
This crap is getting too deep.
I was just supposed to - congratulate you
For completing this major leap.
So, congratulations, Lori -
We wish you all of the best.
Life is full of many challenges,
And I'm sure you can pass the test.

MIRANDA MAE

Miranda Mae - what do you say,
Now that you're learning to talk?
You seem to get into most everything,
Now that you've learned to walk.
But long before you could do either of these
You managed to let us know
How much you loved us, by the way that you hugged us
With your little pat on our backs, just so.
Miranda Mae - just watching you play
Causes our hearts to flutter in awe.
We simply rejoice at the sound of your voice
When you call us Mom Maw and Paw Paw.
Our hearts will swell whenever you're near;
We love to have you around.
Today I feel a special need
To get my pen and write this down.
Miranda Mae - we have something to say,
To the most precious little gal we know:
You are Mom Maw's and Paw Paw's pride and joy,
We take great pleasure in watching you grow.
We dare not attempt to give you this now,
For you'd scribble it up with my pen.
You will get this at an appropriate time
To remind you of us, back then.
Miranda Mae - it'll be O.K.
For we'll be traveling to a better place,
To a far distant world to join family and friends;
To meet "Our Savior" face to face.
As a baby when you told us you loved us,
Sweetheart - we wrote this just for you,
To let you know how special you are
And that we'll always love you, too.

Mom Maw and Paw Paw

SHARON

We just want to let you know
How special you are Sharon Faye.
You're our favorite story teller,
Do you have any good ones today?
You always brighten up the room
Whenever you are near.
We'd like to wish you the very best
With lots of Christmas cheer.
We're looking forward to those big hugs
That you always have for Sue and me.
We'll try not to keep you all to ourselves;
We do have a large family.
We look forward to all family gatherings,
Especially this one today.
We just want to let you know
How special you are, Sharon Faye.

With All Our Love,
Tom and Sue

NO

Once upon a time, I remember when
My sweetheart simply loved me so.
No matter what I wanted or asked her to do,
She would never say no.
Something major has changed o'er the years
That I can't understand feasibly.
She can now say no without explanation,
And she can say no - so easily.

KAITLYN GENTRY

Did we have an angel among us for a while?
There wasn't a prejudiced bone in her body.
Was she sent here as an example for us to see
Ourselves as cliquish, selfish and naughty?
Kaitlyn Gentry was friendly to everyone,
Willing to help anyone, however she could.
As long as it was morally right to do,
If she could help you, she would.
She was so proud of her Uncle Lonnie,
She smiles now at him from above.
She's so happy to see him active in church
And showing others his care and love.
Many have improved their lives from her passing;
Some must always learn the hard way.
The entire Little Miami School District
Is a much closer-knit community, today.
Losing Kaitlyn is such a tragedy for us,
But we should give the Good Lord some slack,
He must have just loaned us "His Special Angel,"
We shouldn't blame Him for wanting her back.

GIFT GIVING

We grew up in the country on a small farm,
And we didn't know we were poor.
Because our parents knew how to live off the land,
We had plenty to eat for sure.
Most of our neighbors were small farmers, too,
So the bulk of us kids were in the same boat.
Very few of us ever got a birthday gift,
Spending was for necessities and to keep farms afloat.
But Mom would remember everyone's birthday
And she'd always bake us a cake.
And our whole family would sing Happy Birthday;
We didn't need gifts to make us feel great.
I've grown much older and a little bit wiser,
And I've watched gift giving get out of hand.
Many spend more than they can afford,
And that can't leave one feeling too grand.
Christmas giving has grown truly outrageous;
Have we forgotten what Christmas is?
We've allowed retailers to brainwash our thinking
To increase their sales for big biz.
I'm cutting back on my spending this year
And I wonder how many this pleases.
We'll have a nice dinner - bake a big cake, and sing
---"Happy Birthday to Jesus." ---

Merry Christmas

My "Dear Mother" left this world 12-17-94

DESTINATION HAPPINESS

Why are you being so mean, Boudine,
To your mother who loves you so much?
Why blame me for everything
Whenever we're in touch?
I've tried hard to do for you
Whatever, whenever I can.
Blaming me for this tragedy
Is something I don't understand.
Imagine yourself as the train engineer
With happiness as your destination.
The engineer must weigh his facts accurately
To get there without hesitation.
If he tries to disguise an obvious problem,
Knowing deep down what's really at fault,
He'll never get there - no matter where -
And more problems will be the result.
You've been on the wrong track lately
Because happiness isn't there any longer.
But with a new map you might soon find
Where happiness grows even stronger.
If unable to put the blame where it belongs,
You could cause your train to derail.
This destination is far too important
To ever allow it to fail.
I've been trying - and still want to help you;
Your happiness is my biggest concern.
We've both made mistakes in the past,
And mistakes are good ways to learn.
Mother needs to hear some loving words from you,
Please try to give her some slack.
For the engineer to reach his destination,
He must be sure to get on the right track.

BRUCE

Bruce was no Casey, that was easy to see,
Getting him was thought a mistake.
But Helen showed patience to the brute
And somehow he turned out just great.
In the beginning he had many faults;
Didn't seem to have common sense.
Later he'd shown a mind of his own
And we knew that he wasn't that dense.
He would get so vigorously excited,
And seemed utterly starved for attention,
But Helen made sure he got plenty of that,
More than there's time here to mention.
They would take regular walks together,
Sometimes they'd hike rather far.
Both enjoyed each other's company,
She'd even take him with her in the car.
A wonderful friendship developed,
A friendship that passed the ultimate test.
He was so trusting right to the end,
Knowing she'd do whatever was best.
I wonder - is there a doggy heaven,
Or must they still on their master depend?
Is he playing with Rags and Casey now,
Or is he waiting for his best friend?

DAVID WAYNE PHILHOWER

I've been told that something good
Will always come from a terrible tragedy.
I've been praying to get some help with this one,
But haven't heard from "His Majesty."
About the worst thing that could possibly happen, did.
A Philhower, only eighteen, needlessly passed away.
It's a dreadful shame that our own David Wayne
Is no longer among us today.
What kind of good can come out of this?
It's a tough one to figure for me.
Within a week since Dave was put to rest,
Two more local families had the same tragedy.
I wonder, could "Almighty God" be asking us
To wake up to the local drug problem per se?
Could "He" be singling out some special ones,
Trying to get our attention some way?
Is "He" telling us that we've been too relaxed
By putting up with what's right in front of our eyes;
Seeing big money made on illegal drugs,
And watch while another family cries?
We've allowed this problem to become so huge
By not wanting to be seen or known as a rat;
But to let these dealers continue to prey on us
Is considerably worse than that.
Could "The Good Lord" have us in his plan
To answer prayers in our neighborhood?
I've been thinking about this quite a bit
As if so, David can show us some good.
When "The Big Guy Upstairs" picked him to serve,
To help with a problem down here
And caused us to do what "He" wants us to,
We should give David our cheer.
Don't get me wrong, Dave was no angel,
But we truly loved him, and he is sorely missed.
I'm asking this community to pull together right now
And make something good come of this.

OLD AGE

When the body aches from old wounds
Or another body part wears out,
Moaning and groaning just annoys others,
And it doesn't help to cuss or shout.
My big sister is a good example
Of how one should handle this.
She can accept whatever comes up
And appear to turn hell into bliss.
I don't have time in this little rhyme
To describe all that she's been through.
But briefly, to make my point
I'll mention here just a few.
She's almost blind from macular degeneration;
Has had one of her kidneys removed.
But she tries to think positively
On how things might be improved.
Most of her worries are about others,
Those who she loves so dear.
Her grandchildren's health and happiness
Is now her greatest fear.
She has the right attitude to endure old age,
And one must be tough to get there.
She doesn't hesitate to speak her own mind,
Especially to doctors who don't seem to care.
When I heard that her only kidney had failed,
I asked her, "Is dialysis causing you strife?"
She smiled at me and said casually,-
"It's just another change of life."

CAREER WOMAN OR MOTHER

I'm so proud of my daughter Lori,
Who graduated from an excellent college;
But she wouldn't allow her good education
To diminish her common sense knowledge.
She had plans for a promising career,
But that changed shortly after marriage.
In less than a year she was a mother,
On her continuing work, opinions varied.
She decided that being a mother was more important.
And she gave it some thought, she's nobody's fool.
She uses her education and is still learning
With five kids now in Home School.
She has time to raise them correctly;
They sometimes even get spanked when they've done wrong.
And the whole family is active in church,
(Maybe I should be writing a song.)
Most career women drop the kids off at day care
Rushing to climb "that ladder" to a successful career,
Expecting to make it quickly and stay on top;
And it takes most all of their time, thought, effort and cheer.
Sometimes the worst possible thing that could happen, does,
With a job that keeps them constantly on the run.
Might even forget to stop at the day care
And leave the baby locked in the car, in the sun.
Motherhood should never be handled too lightly,
And now, more than ever, I'm proud of my Lori.
And I want her to know that she made the right choice.
Her kids are on "the top rung," above career and glory.

BARB AND ANN

I'm sure neither of you realize
How much you have helped me lately,
Being so caring to a lowly P.R.N.
A peon that's not at all stately,
For me, everything seems to be going wrong,
And I've been weighted down with depression.
You two make me feel like I matter,
And have helped to reverse my regression.
You not only bought me groceries,
But you even did a lot of my work.
I haven't done anything to deserve your help,
But you pitched in when I was hurt.
Showing me that you really do care
Brings a big tear to my eye.
Knowing you're not looking for a pat on the back,
Simply your kindness is making me cry.
I wish more people could be like you.
I plan to help others whenever I can.
This isn't much - but I'm trying to thank you,
My now good friends - Barb and Ann.

Thank You So Much
Love, Phyllis

KEITH GORDON

Keith always says, "Good morning, Tom"
At Speedway, when I stop for my coffee refill.
If it's too busy for others to speak,
There's no doubt in my mind that he will.
I'll ask, "How are you this morning, Keith?"
And I know what he'll have to say.
He'll spit it out quickly, "I'm miserable,"
But he doesn't say it in a miserable way.
Jim was quite upset with Keith
When he had to take off to go to court.
Charged with assault for jacking his doctor's jaw,
Thinking the doctor used him for sport.
When he was asked, "How do you plea?"
He said, "Guilty your honor, but I had cause."
The judge replied, "I can't wait to hear this."
And stared at Keith with a pause.
"I did put 'the whammy' on the doctor
With my fist up side of his head.
I do have a bit of a temper,
But I misunderstood what he said."
"Your honor, he told me with his finger in my face:
'To get well, you should be a vegetarian.'
But I thought he told me to go to hell
And I should see a veterinarian."
The judge couldn't help but giggle somewhat
And he just had to let him off easy.
Keith is behind the counter this morning
Chewing Tums 'cause his tummy is queasy.
When I walked in he said, "Good morning, Tom."
And then started mumbling to stir up the peace.
As I listened to him and filled my cup to the brim
I asked, "How are you this morning, Keith?"

MERRY CHRISTMAS, SWEETHEART

No gift for you from me to go under the tree,
Sweetheart, for that I'm ashamed.
And I can't come up with a legitimate excuse,
And there's no one else to be blamed.
I should have had something for you tucked away,
In case times like these came along.
But I'm a dimwit and didn't plan ahead.
My brain just isn't that strong.
No present wrapped in pretty paper,
Sealed and tied with a bow.
But I do have something for you
And Sweetheart, it continues to grow.
No, I'm not speaking of Wally,
You know he's weakening and shrinking in size.
Let's try to use our vivid imaginations
To keep that old boy alive.
My gift for you is "the love in my heart,"
It swells bigger and stronger each day.
Love that has been there for a number of years,
And Sweetheart - it's there to stay.
I'm writing this to give you a little something;
It's not much, but it's all I can do.
And I wish you a very "Merry Christmas,"
And Sweetheart, I'll always love you.

Merry Christmas, my Love

And

Happy Birthday to Jesus

OLD FRIENDS

Don't take old friends for granted,
I must tell you something about them.
Really good friends are hard to come by,
And it's tough to live without them.
A true friend will give you assistance
Whenever you might need a hand.
And you don't even mind asking,
Because they'll want to help you, if they can.
Someone who, you'll want to help, too,
Whenever they feel the need to ask.
Assisting good friends is enjoyable
And it's seldom a major task.
My best friends were all older than me,
But we enjoyed our time together.
No matter whose project we'd be working on,
The more we teased each other, the better.
Now I'm giving my old buddies hell
Because they've left this world without me.
I would guess they're looking down now
And laughing at what they know about me.
I don't suppose it'll be very long
Until we may be together again.
I didn't imagine I'd miss them so much,
There's such a void being without them.

CHARLIE PHILHOWER

I understand you're quite the "ladies man,"
Even at eighty years old.
You still walk tall and flirt with them all,
At least that's what I've been told.
Golfing and hunting are second and third
Of your favorite things to do.
You're an example for others to follow,
And we all look up to you.
You've always been a man of honor,
I've heard this from those who know you best.
Is that why you sit at the head of the table
At Newtonsville's Gathering Place of rest?
After we sang "Happy Birthday" to Charlie,
You had some words of wisdom to give:
"May I live as long as I want to,
And may I want to, as long as I live."
I wish you could see what I have imagined,
I think you would find it pleasant.
It's you using a five iron to get out of the rough
And bringing down a ring-necked pheasant.
And returning home to your sweetheart
To share with her all of the fun
Of making the shot of a lifetime,
Even better than "a hole in one."

WE'VE BEEN BLESSED

Janice, I must say that you have impressed me
By not seeming to be too concerned.
You certainly didn't sound like you were wearing a frown,
On the phone saying your house had just burned.
While telling me your home and its contents were a total loss,
You didn't seem at all distressed.
You were so thankful that everyone got out okay,
Saying, "We have been truly blessed."
I know how hard you and Dick worked,
To get your place so comfortable and nice,
Then burned to ash and turned to trash,
Appeared to be a horrible price.
But you had the "Good Lord" on your side,
Making this tragedy much easier to take.
To figure "He" will do what's best for you,
You had faith in "Him," for heaven's sake.
If the fire would have happened an hour earlier
You may have all died in your sleep.
We must thank "Our Savior" for blessing us all,
Our souls are his to keep.
You said you're receiving lots of gifts,
Others giving to help you survive.
Even your insurance company put things in high gear;
So many are thankful that you're still alive.
You feel you may come out of this better than you were;
It's amazing what "The Lord" can do.
When you can put your trust and faith totally in "Him,"
"He" will take care of you.
You and Dick have your faith in the right place;
Me, you have certainly impressed.
You have shown me, and others will see,
That you have been "truly blessed."

FAMILY GATHERINGS

It's so good to be together again today
To enjoy another family gathering.
Are you showing your best social graces,
By flattering more than battering?
All families have their quarrels and spats
Causing one to feel like another doesn't care.
But deep down within, we know that our kin,
When needed, will always be there.
Family ties are where true love lies
And true love is what binds this family so tight.
When we get together, the more the better,
We can make bad times a little more bright.
These little ones here with their sparkle of joy,
Can touch the softest spot in my heart.
They have a way to make my day
And I think of them often, when we're apart.
Most of us here have fully matured
Even though we may not always show it.
We're all capable of acting childish for fun,
But we try not to let the little ones know it.
We truly miss our loved ones who've passed on,
That void can cause a frown.
We pray that they're in a better place now,
And that their elevator didn't go down.
I try not to miss family gatherings;
We have no promise for tomorrow.
I want to enjoy all of you, as long as I can,
(Do you have any money I might borrow?)
All joking aside, you're all precious to me,
Family love is stronger than any other.
And there's no closer bond than mother and child -

Happy Birthday, Mother!

MOTHERLY LOVE

A good mother develops "motherly love"
That swells within, before she ever gives birth.
This "motherly love" continues to grow
As she quenches her newborn's hunger and thirst.
She'll clean and care for the baby;
Rock and sing it to sleep.
And she will protect it with her own life,
And make you watch your language when you speak.
She won't be a friend to the youngsters,
She will play with them often, just so,
But she knows that she is the mother
And must take charge and often say no.
A good mother assumes responsibility
For teaching before and after school.
Always leading by proper example
And following the Golden Rule.
"Motherly love" is an everlasting love
That can withstand many faults.
A love from somewhere with such special care,
Still growing when all are adults.
Even grown-ups need a good mother's love,
They know who cares for them most.
She is the one that they can lean on,
When they're down - with a really bad dose.
This "motherly love" is a gift from above,
Sometimes it's needed to understand.
And when there's no one else willing to help,
She's there to give a helping hand.
There's no stronger love than "motherly love,"
A good mother's love is so true.
Sometimes we seem hateful, but we're truly grateful
To have such a good mother as YOU.

SCOOTER

Scooter had already gathered the eggs
And was helping Auntie Cheryl feed the critters,
When the bantam rooster attacked the three year old;
Then Uncle Squiggy grilled some chicken fritters.
Scooter has a knack for finding a snack,
So we try to keep an eye on the squirt.
We must coax her to eat her dinner
Before she gets ice cream or dessert.
Uncle Squiggy, Auntie Cheryl and Scooter
When cruising will stop at favorite spots,
It's pretty much taken for granted
That scooter must have her "ring-pops."
No doubt she gets spoiled a bit,
They are partners, three of a kind.
When the sun begins to set, you can bet
They'll have the same thing on their mind.
Driving around the fields to watch the deer,
This is their favorite game.
Scooter knows the way and where they stay;
I'd bet she can call them by name.
She'll come running to me with binoculars in hand,
Thinking she'll see a really big buck.
Yelling "Pawpaw! Papaw! It's deer-thirty,
Do you care if we take your truck?"
She likes to sit on the padded armrest
So she's level with Cheryl and Squiggy.
Then she'll use both hands to gaze o'er the land
Hoping to spot "the biggie."
When they return and it's almost bedtime;
Scooter will bring me some goodies.
She'll climb up in my chair for us to share
Something good, like Oreo cookies.

MR. WILLIAMS

I went to visit Mr. Williams today,
I hadn't seen him for way too long.
He's still the same fine gentleman as always
Even though he's not quite as strong.
You wouldn't believe it by looking,
But he is ninety years old.
He can still out walk me considerably
And his personality has never grown cold.
He has kept his great sense of humor
And he keeps a smile on his face.
If all human kind had his frame of mind,
We wouldn't have problems with race.
As we were conversing and reminiscing
I needed to thank him for all he has done.
He made growing up in this rural community
Much more pleasant and fun.
He was our Cub Scout leader
And he helped coach the baseball team.
He'd let me hunt, trap and fish on his place,
He could make his neighbors' lights beam.
He showed me pictures of his high school class;
Lockland in nineteen thirty eight.
He was on both the track and football teams,
He didn't say it, but I'll bet he was great.
His son Lee was a leader in my class,
I'm sure he's tried to follow in his Dad's steps.
But I know of one place that Lee fell short
And I feel there he may have regrets.

Mr. Williams showed me his graduation picture
And he was a dashingly handsome young man.
I said, "Gee! You're much better looking than Lee."
He grinned saying, "Tell Sonny that when you can."
We both giggled knowing this as the truth.
But seriously - all joking aside,
Mr. Williams you have always been an honorable man,
You can hold your head high with pride.
You've always worked hard and you know how to play.
I pray that you continue to enjoy the rest of your days.
And thanks to a few "good men" like you
Some of us learn the right ways.

Thanks again,
Tommy

PAP

I'm spending the day with Pap again,
We like to help each other when we can.
It seems that whenever we get together
We have a good time, man to man.
We simply enjoy each other's company;
It's been said that we make a good team.
I don't remember what we were doing this time
When I was awakened from my dream.
Then realizing that it's been over twenty years
Since Pap passed away.
But we still have a good time - in my mind,
He's etched in my heart and thoughts to stay.
When I became Dad I nicknamed him Pap,
We were as close as a father and son could be.
I didn't tell him enough that I loved him,
But he knew it, and I knew he loved me.
When I was a lad calling him Dad
He was so worthy of my respect.
He was always there with his wisdom to share,
And none of us felt any neglect.
Family was his top priority;
He was quite a role model to follow.
I wish my kids could look up to me, as well,
But compared to him, I feel hollow.
Whenever something was bothering any of us,
He'd know it and he could appease it.
No matter how bad a problem might be,
He'd have something to say to ease it.
Pap was so down to earth, but a brilliant man
Who always knew just what to say.
I hope I get to spend more time with him, -
I love you Pap - "Happy Father's Day."

Wayne

CELEBRATING A LIFE

Joan Lynn Green
November 18, 1963 – November 19, 2009

When my Joni lost her life,
I didn't think that I could handle it.
But with Tim's precious love and help,
I'm now able to keep my candle lit.
Joni was my first born,
And eventually we became best friends.
I felt that losing her was "the ultimate loss"
But I've learned that our love never ends.
We grew up more like sisters;
I was just a child when she was born.
Our tempers could get riled up a bit,
And at each other we both have sworn.
Joni always made it hard on herself,
Living up to being a dingy blonde.
But she was such a loving person
Who could hold to a special bond.
Just to show you what I mean,
At 12, with the death of her dear friend,
She carried Lisa with herself
Up until the very end.
Seldom is felt that strong of a bond,
No doubt this is quite rare.
But she loved her own family even more,
And to our Lisa, "your mother did care."
Family ties are where true love lies,
But one may take too much for granted.
Looking at life selfishly
Can get the family balance slanted.
A mother's love is everlasting,
Joni and I will never part.
She will always be "right here - with me,
Living - within my mind and heart."

Mom

CHLOE MARIE

Chloe Marie, you're a bundle of glee;
Eight pounds, one ounce, and 21½ inches long.
Born 3:59 A.M., 5-19-10,
Then Mom feeds you and sings you a song.
Chloe Marie, now that you can see,
What do you think of your father and mother?
Right now our need to take care of you
Is much stronger than any other.
Chloe Marie - "golly gee,"
Those gorgeous dark eyes are so bright.
We're now thinking, with government stinking
We've got to do things for you just right.
Chloe Marie, our whole country
Seems to be stumbling down the wrong path.
Families are really getting fed-up
And we're worried how long this can last.
Chloe Marie, how will your life be
When you are our age and older?
We must do whatever we need to
And make ourselves stronger and bolder.
Chloe Marie, we'll start early
Saving for, and planning your schooling.
And we'll try to be who you can look up to,
And guide you with proper ruling.
Chloe Marie, you may be "the key,"
That locks us closer together.
Could you be the "calm after the storm,"
Bringing us much better weather?
Chloe Marie, you have truly
Changed the way that we think.
I wish our government could change as well,
So there wouldn't be near as much stink.

JOHNSON FAMILY REUNION

Our Johnson family reunion
Is always a real treat.
There are ten of us with our offspring,
And we hillbillies know how to eat.
We've dotted the countryside far and wide,
No longer on the same side of the hill.
"Hillbilly, Ridge-Runner, Buckeye or Briar" -
We're close knit kinfolk, still.
We men may drink and brag a bit
While tending the slow cooking briskets.
The ladies do up the taters, chicken and dumplings,
And bake the pies, cakes and biscuits.
It's a dreadful shame to lose the Johnson name,
When our gals wed and take on a new label.
But in-laws and outlaws, we all get along
When around the family supper table.
I've been noticing the past few years,
Much more obvious here, recently,
The original ten and spouses now kin
Are all getting old but me.

Jim

LIMSMURFF

Stopping for coffee at Speedway
Is my daily routine.
They have the best and freshest brew
And I do need my caffeine.
Being a regular customer,
I call the employees by name.
And I usually try to be a nice guy,
And expect to be treated the same.
This morning Limsmurff was at the register
Shaking her head back and forth.
I had no idea what the problem was,
But she kept shaking it, south to north.
I walked by to the coffee pots
And refilled my big cup,
Then proceeded to the register
To find out what was up.
Asking, "How are you this morning?"
Thinking it might help her to chat.
Then she said, still shaking her head,
"I'm peachy, fine as a frog hair, HOW'S THAT?"

NOTHING FOR ME

When I come home from a hard day's work
There are things I look forward to,
Like plopping down in my easy chair
To enjoy a western or two.
But when the grandkids come over
My habits will change a bit.
They like to tease me whenever they can,
And don't know when to quit.
When it comes to dealing with Pa-Paw,
Miranda just five and Evan but two,
They can team to quickly scheme
And I'm never sure what they will do.
When I came home yesterday
I heard the pitter-patter of little feet.
I thought they were running to give me a hug
But that would've been too neat.
They were racing to get into Pa-Paw's chair
Already watching SpongeBob on my T.V.
And they're sharing my favorite snacks
But won't give any to me.
The Evanator comes up with his comment
As he walks over to me, strutting.
With his mouth full of cashews he said:
"Pa-Paw - You haven't got no nothing."

DADDY'S LITTLE GIRL

You were kind of homely when just born,
Fuzzy hair without any curl.
And your loud bellow was not at all mellow,
Can this be - "Daddy's Little Girl?"
I couldn't handle changing diapers
And I wouldn't clean house or cook.
Raising babies is women's work,
That was the law in my book.
Your Mother deserves all the credit;
Putting up with me, she is a pearl.
I was a jerk, letting her do the work,
For your brothers and - "Daddy's Little Girl."
I didn't spend enough time with you kids,
Selfishly doing other things.
If I could relive my life I would relieve some strife,
For this I would certainly change.
You learned to walk and talk rather quickly
So you and Michael could quarrel.
Big brother was shown you could hold your own,
When spatting with - "Daddy's Little Girl."
You were only four when Brian arrived,
And you wanted to feed the little guy.
You weren't big enough to hold him alone,
But you had to give it a try.
You held and gave him his bottle
As we watched you give it a whirl.
Me and your mother smiled at each other
As Brian was fed by - "Daddy's Little Girl."
That same year you got lost in Krogers
While shopping with Granny and Mom.
We felt our hearts burst as we feared the worst,
Thinking a pervert had you under his palm.
Uncle Don found you five hours later
In Gramp's junk car, asleep, rolled up in a curl
Two miles away, and you made it O.K.
God was watching over - "Daddy's Little Girl."

You went with me once to check turtle lines
And we caught one on the very first jug.
As I carried it along, humming a song,
You came running from behind to give me a hug.
As you hugged my leg the turtle bit you,
Causing both my temper and knife to swirl.
But you got the last bite, that very night
It was dinner for "Daddy's Little Girl."
You're a chip off the ol' block in softball,
Learning all the facets of the game.
And you'd do whatever it took to win,
Even when it caused you some pain.
Those belly slides had to hurt,
And your arm, you could really hurl.
When you'd hit the ball, clear to the wall,
That was "Daddy's Little Girl."
Lori Ann, you grew up too fast;
Wasn't long till you were calling me wimp.
I'm hoping you might ease up a bit
And won't start calling me gimp.
I drag my feet now when I walk,
I'm just short, I'm not in a furrow.
And you may be taller than me,
But you're still "Daddy's Little Girl."

You graduated from a fine college,
So you could home-school your kids.
That sixth one made that job too big;
I'm glad that you're over that bridge.
Such a large family keeps you active,
Many important projects to twirl.
You're now grown with a man of your own.
But you're still "Daddy's Little Girl."
We should try to see more of each other,
It seems we always have too much to do.
The older I get, the more I fret;
I haven't told you enough, "I LOVE YOU."
You know that I'm a homebody,
I spend most of my time in this borough.
But I'll love you Lori, till the end of my story.
Because you're "Daddy's Little Girl."

MICHELLE

Michelle is like the "Energizer Bunny,"
She keeps going, and going, and going.
Always plugging away, day after day
With pain growing, and growing, and growing.
She gets up early every morning,
Trying not to let anyone down.
Devotedly caring for the elderly,
Helping a smile to replace a frown.
Michelle has always been a worker,
Holding two jobs is her status quo;
Wanting to be shut off and running her butt off,
But there's plenty more left there to go.
Up early on Saturdays and Sundays too,
With her eyes somewhat rosy,
Afraid she might miss out on something.
The actual truth is: she's nosey.
She looks forward to those weekends
Meeting with friends to party.
Don't play any joke with her rum and Coke
And try to short her on Bacardi.
Michelle has a great sense of humor
And she loves to have a good time.
But she won't hesitate to set you straight
If you happen to get out of line.
Sometimes she gets rather boisterous
And unintentionally may cause a distraction.
She's just naturally loud and when in a crowd
Automatically becomes the attraction.
When the weekend is on the downside
And most of the fun is done,
She knows she'll still be hurting tomorrow
And will again be on the run.
With battery recharged and agony enlarged,
She'll work with pain flaring, and flaring, and flaring.
Helping the elderly smile, for their last little while,
Because she's so caring, and caring, and caring.

FAMILY PHOTOS

Family photos can be valuable treasures,
Memories to share and cherish from the past.
Notations must be put on the back
For the truth of those moments to last.
Old photos, without documentation,
May cause arguments within the family.
Sometimes there's more than one claiming:
"That's definitely a picture of me!"
Some avoid having their picture taken,
While others want to put on a big show.
Are you afraid you might break the camera,
Or do you feel that your photos will glow?
Most children love to have theirs taken
And they'll make faces and dream up games.
While everything is still fresh in your mind,
Be sure to print details, date and names.
School pictures are a must for all of us,
Especially early grades and graduations.
And we must not forget to have the flash set
For church functions and special occasions.
Wedding pictures are so delightful
With the lovely bride and handsome groom.
Lots of good shots follow at the reception
And some during breaks on the honeymoon.
I love to take pictures of the kids three and under;
They're nearly always in a natural setting.
They seldom run, hide or pose,
And you can never be sure what you're getting.
To obtain a look at some family members
For later generations to share,
You must sneak around and not make a sound
And shoot while they don't know you're there.
If you should inherit good family photos
With names and dates known to be true,
You might realize that the "old fogeys" now
Were once - a whole lot like you.

STARLIGHT

The light of a star shines continually
Even if only seen at night.
It's always there, shining somewhere,
For someone to enjoy the sight.
I stop at Thornton's every morning
To get my coffee refill, feeling grim.
I limp, in low gear, with little or no cheer
And fill up my cup to the brim;
Tasting it, before I go to the counter,
To be sure it was brewed just right.
I'm getting familiar with most of the help,
And one of them really shines bright.
I spoke to her this morning saying,
"You always seem to be in a good mood."
She replied, "It's my fine family, healthy kids,
And I'm so happy with no need to brood.
I'm quite content with what I have,
With very much to be thankful for."
She's right, many of us are never satisfied,
Always wanting and looking for more.
I asked her name and she said, "Starlight,
But most everyone calls me Star."
I thought to myself what a beautiful name
And so fitting for who you are.
For the light of a star shines continually
Whether at work or at play.
This lovely Starlight shines not only at night,
For she just naturally brightens my day.

JASON WHITAKER, BIG GAME HUNTER

Jason Whitaker wanted to give deer huntin' a shot
And asked Bobby, "Would you mind if I tag along?"
Bobby didn't want him to go, but couldn't say no,
Thinkin' Jason might take it wrong.
So he said, "O.K., but not today;
There's a lot of stuff to get that you'll need.
I'll make you a list, but I must insist
That we leave at five in the mornin', agreed?"
Surprisingly, Jason was ready to go
When Bobby stopped in front of his house.
And then it hit him: No breakfast!
So he stuffed cookies in his pockets and mouth.
He didn't short himself any on huntin' gear,
He even took along a cell phone,
And had his wife call every ten minutes -
He didn't feel safe in the dark, all alone.
Bobby put him in his favorite spot,
Then walked on to another tree stand.
Not expectin' much from his younger brother,
But Jason proved to be more than he'd planned.
Evidently the phone ringin' in the dark
Didn't cause the deer any fear.
For at the first hint of daybreak
Jason was surrounded by deer!
When he raised his gun up to shoot one
They scattered in every direction.
Then his gun barrel swells till he runs out of shells,
For his aim was short of perfection.
He'd been braggin' to Bobby on bein' a good shot,
Trap shootin' for some time every week.
This may sound queer, but when he shot at those deer
All he hit was the land owner's Jeep.

Needless to say, this was the last day
That Bobby took Jason deer huntin'.
But it don't seem to bother Jason at all;
See if you don't think this is somethin':
Jason takes pride in that deer hunt,
At least that's what I've heard said.
He admires that Jeep mounted on the wall
Much more than any deer head.

MATT MAUPIN

When a loved one joins the military
And gets sent off to war,
We pray for the best, but fear the worst
Not knowing what the Good Lord has in store.
Can you imagine what Matt's loved ones went through
When they saw him bound and displayed on TV;
With terrorists threatening his death, and impossible requests,
Fearing he might be the next casualty?
And then not hearing anything for years,
While holding candlelight vigils and prayers,
Knowing it would take a miracle to get him back now,
From the "Big Guy" upstairs.
But Keith and Carolyn were so proud of Matt,
That they refused to give up hope.
And encouraged other military families
To faithfully support our troops, and not mope.
Well, now the waiting is over
And our prayers weren't answered this time.
Matt isn't coming home safely, as we wished,
And his death is a brutal crime.
It's impossible for us to understand
How God could allow it to happen this way.
But we must trust that He knows best,
And this will turn out O.K.
I believe that He may have used Matt
To make this a better place to live.
I know we have a closer community now,
With many more willing to give.
Matt's remains are coming home soon;
Lots of yellow ribbons to show the way.
He'll be getting quite a welcoming, as he's put to rest,
And there'll be more to learn from this, someday.

The Good Lord sometimes uses soldiers
To get civilian lame-brains' attention.
Many simply take our freedom for granted,
It's a shame that this I must mention.
But there is nothing free about the cost of freedom;
Freedom comes at a terrible price.
For Iraq to ever gain true freedom,
Good soldiers like Matt must lose their lives.
And it's a shame that good troops have to die
For us to realize the sacrifices they've made.
Then how do we honor most of them? -
With a brief Memorial Day parade.
I don't want to take anything away from Matt;
He certainly deserves all the praise he's gotten.
But even when warriors come home alive
We should honor them BIG - like we'll do with Matt Maupin.
Yes, Matt will continue to serve Our Father above,
While he'll be missed immensely by all of us here.
And Keith and Carolyn – Matt is so proud of you,
I'm sure he sends you his cheer.

SOMETIMES

Sometimes I wonder if you love me.
Sometimes I know that you do.
Sometimes I think my heart will break
Because I do love you.
Sometimes when you want to be with me
You'll let nothing stand in your way.
Sometimes you avoid me like the plague;
How will you feel, today?
Sometimes I'm sure things just happen
When neither of us is at fault.
Sometimes I'm sure you make up excuses
To bring our meeting to a halt.
Sometimes I wonder what will come of us,
That's why I've written you these lines.
But what makes my life worth living most
Is you - loving me - sometimes.

HAPPY MOTHER'S DAY, SWEETHEART

A good "Mother's love" is so special,
It's difficult to be explained.
It's not taught or learned, bought or earned,
It's just there, and can't be restrained.
Sweetheart, you are such a good mom,
Teaching the kids as you care for them.
Even when grown, thinking they're out on their own,
They know when needed, you'll be there for them.
I can't put into lines all of the times
I've noticed the things that you've done.
Sacrifices you've made to show you're top grade,
And as a mother, you're "number one."
I can easily see, the kids come before me;
I understand, it shouldn't be any other way.
I love the kids, too, but I'm in love with you.
Sweetheart - - - Happy Mother's Day!

TO ABBY,
FROM MAMMOO AND POPADO

Abby, today is not your birthday.
It's not a holiday of any kind.
We'd like to say on this ordinary day
That you're "so special" - all of the time.
You absolutely brighten up our lives.
We love it when you come over here.
Every day, in your own sweet way,
You give us so very much cheer.
But you are growing up so fast,
We need to hurry and tell you true
How much you really mean to us,
Your Mammoo and Papado.
Someday, when you get to be our age
And have great grand kids of your own,
You might want to show them this picture
And share with them this poem.
And tell them about your childhood
And all the things we used to do,
And pass along fond memories
Of your Mammoo and Papado

DEBBIE'S DRIVING RECORD

Before Debbie joined up with King's Automall,
Her driving record was clear as a bubble.
Being put on the run to get everything done,
She now often runs into trouble.
She actually drove up a flight of stairs,
Swerving to miss a concrete truck,
Claiming that load took up the whole road
And there was nowhere to go, but up!
That was pretty good, but not the best:
Still trying to get all her errands done
She made a huge mistake while running late;
The pressure had her under the gun.
She hurriedly drove into a new parking lot
And dropped into wet concrete.
Needless to say, this wasn't her day
And the concrete finisher looked bleak.
He stood there aghast with his mouth wide open
While Debbie's was running with plenty to say,
Complaining about no signs like "KEEP OUT!"
And no detour to show another way!
She used language stronger than normal,
For her temper just had to explode.
The concrete man takes all he can
And then - HE starts to unload.

While he's giving her a piece of his mind,
Debbie's gritting her teeth thinking, "Whatever."
Then realizing if she doesn't get out of there,
She could be stuck in concrete forever.
So, instead of backing out a few feet,
She made her point to get his attention.
She quickly shot across the whole lot
While being called names I can't even mention.
She still claims to be a good driver
As she explains her last wreck to the cops:
"Officers, I had that yellow light made
If that idiot in front hadn't stopped."
Debbie's now on a first name basis
With body shops trying to save her some cash.
Insurance companies have written her off
And we have nicknamed her "Crash."

SAMMIE BOY

Our friend Terry tried to find a home
For his runt of the litter Beagle pup.
It appeared he was bound to go to the pound
Because nobody wanted the mutt.
Then dad had visions of a free hunting dog
And gave him a home and a name.
But the little guy got truly gun shy
And was afraid to play that shooting game.
Sammie Boy was a disappointment for dad
And he acted like an old "fuddy duddy."
But Gladys loved him at first sight
And he became her best buddy.
They would take long walks together
As Sammy Boy would follow a scent.
And as long as no gun shots went off
Nobody would ever get bent.
He became a real family member
With adopted cats as sisters and brothers.
But Sammie Boy ruled the roost,
Feeling he was the "king" of the others.
Jeff, Grace and little Angel
Loved to walk and play with him, too.
And now he's no longer with us,
What are we going to do?

I know Sammie Boy got on your nerves, dad,
As he barked and kept you awake.
But I know, deep down, that you loved him;
After all, he was your namesake.
I wonder, what's the little guy doing now?
Could somebody give me a hint?
Is there an afterlife for little Beagles?
Is he trailing a heavenly scent?
I'd like to believe he is better off now,
And I'll try to tell you why.
Even though we have tears, he's shed all his fears
And I'll bet he's no longer gun shy.
I have written this hoping to help with the loss,
And thanks, dad, you kept him out of the pound,
Giving him a full life with very little strife;
Leaving fond memories - of our little hound.

WEZIE

I've always been an outdoorsman,
Camo is my normal wear.
Those who know me have grown used to it
And anymore, they don't even stare.
I stop for coffee on the way to work,
A thirty two ounce mug refill.
I clown around with customers I've never met;
It's tough for me to keep still.
As I get back in my truck to pull out,
A car pulled in front of me and stopped.
Wondering - Is someone angry at me?
As my heart and lower jaw dropped.
I got out of my truck and walked over
To see a little sweet lady smile at me.
She just wanted to say, "You've made my day
With your natural smile and being so friendly."
I asked her name and she replied,
"Everyone just calls me Wezie."
I didn't dare ask how she came up with that
For the answer may not have been easy.
Her comment caused me to feel wonderful,
For I was only being myself,
And to learn that some do - appreciate you
For what you are, is really true wealth.

Well, Wezie, I want to thank YOU
For giving your time to make my day.
I'm proud of you for who you are
And I have something else to say:
You and I are both happy people;
Joy doesn't come from being hateful or cruel.
I hope others can learn from our example
And follow the "Golden Rule."
Wezie, I question why you stopped me,
Your answer may explain it all.
Did you think I was Santa Claus in camouflage
Because I'm not very tall?
Well, Wezie, I hate to disappoint you,
But I have no reindeer or sleigh.
Yes, I'm short with a pot belly and white beard,
And I hope my smile is here to stay.

Merry Christmas, Wezie!

MY SOLID FOUNDATION

FOND MEMORIES
OF MOM AND DAD

Fond memories of Mom and Dad
Are sealed within me to stay.
I never once doubted their love,
And I'll see them again some day.
I grew up with true loving care,
Church on Sunday and summer Bible School,
Being taught how Jesus paid for my sins,
And to follow the "Golden Rule."
We should treat our fellow man this way,
As we don't want them going to hell.
And we should be examples for all to see,
With testimonies to tell.
My parents lived good Christian lives,
Teaching us kids to do the same.
They would witness to neighbors and friends,
Team players, trying to win the game.
The game of life is most important,
Think of it - "Eternity is forever."
And it's not an easy game to win
Because Satan is so clever.
I've fallen for his temptations,
Even since I have been saved.
I'll put on a show not to let anyone know,
But God knows I've misbehaved.
I'm thankful for His gift of life,
I haven't lost it by running off track.
When Almighty God gives His children a gift,
He's not going to take it back.
God has promised me a place in heaven;
I don't deserve an executive seat.
What I fear most of my poor performance
Is my loved ones may catch the heat.

Imagine eternity in Heaven, knowing
You have loved ones forever in hell.
Never any peace, gnashing of teeth,
I don't think I could handle this well.
The worst possibility for me would be
To know my son or daughter was there,
Because I'd dropped the ball in the game of life.
Please God, don't give me this pain to bear.
Are fond memories of your mother and me
Sealed within you to stay?
Do you know in your heart that when we part
We'll be together again, some day?

I TRY TO TALK TO GOD

Each morning before I go to work
I must say my prayers.
Oh yes, I try to talk to God,
He helps me with my cares.
Sometimes I wonder if He hears.
Sometimes I have a doubt.
But deep down I believe He's hearing me,
And He sees me when I pout.
You're right; I don't go to church,
Though I've done so in the past.
I've tried to do what others say is best,
But for me, it doesn't last.
The preacher will read some scripture
And explain what it means to me.
Another will tell me what the passage means
With a different theology.
How is one to know who's really right
Or to know who's really wrong?
"If you don't believe the way I do,
You'll be in hell, before long."
I like to sleep in Sunday morn',
Get up and take it easy.
I've worked hard most all the week;
Sunday, I'm being lazy.
I know I've sinned; will sin again,
To God I must confess.
I ask him for forgiveness,
And to help me with this mess.
When a loved one is hurt or sick,
I drop down on my knees
And pray to God to make them well.
Have mercy on us, please.

GOD'S HOLY WORD

"In the beginning was the Word,
And the Word was with God, and the Word was God."
God is the Father, the Son, and the Holy Spirit;
Does God being the Word strike you as odd?
How do you really get to know the Word?
By reading and studying the Bible.
The Word is our guide to follow,
The only one that is truly reliable.
The Authorized King James 1611 Bible,
The Word of God - absolutely true.
His almighty hands laid out the plans
To teach us the right things to do.
There is so much to learn in this "Holy Book,"
A wealth of knowledge to be gained.
"Study to shew thyself approved unto God,
A workman that needeth not to be ashamed,
Rightly dividing the word of truth." -
Never change it or you will be blamed!
Many scholars and theologians run off track
When they change or rearrange His Word.
They'll sift through writings in Hebrew and Greek,
But changing God's word is absurd.
God inspired it to be written as He wanted it,
With warnings not to add or take away.
But many scholars looking for dollars
Let Satan lead them astray.
Revelation 5 says it's a seven sealed book,
Sealed within and without.
I'm looking at mine, it was sealed seven times,
And that makes me want to shout!

The Bible, the true word of God,
Wasn't written for scholars and theologians;
But for the common man to understand
And know, if needed, God may part the oceans.
We need to pray often, thanking Jesus, Our Guide,
He paid the full price the way it was done. -
The Father, the Son, the Holy Spirit and the Word,
From the beginning, all have been one.

FELLOWSHIP

Fellowship is a friendly relationship
Existing among two or more people.
I look forward to seeing my friends at church;
There's much fellowship under that steeple.
Why the need for fellowship?
One can get quite lonely without it.
Is this fellowship sincere and real?
Let's just think a minute about it.
The blind can see the care we share
When a brother or sister runs into trouble.
And some will be there to comfort you
When you've stumbled and busted your bubble.
What makes this fellowship truly great
Is what draws us so closely together.
Knowing that Jesus Christ has paid the full price
To cleanse all the sins we have gathered.
We didn't deserve "His Sacrifice,"
No one has ever been worthy of this.
God hates sin - and we're so full of it;
But because He loves us, He gave us this "Gift."
We were created in His own image
For Him to have fellowship with us.
He would walk and talk with Adam and Eve,
Until they betrayed His trust.
We are so fortunate now to be blessed;
Thanks to Jesus, God no longer sees our sin.
For when we're saved, our sins are washed away,
For an everlasting fellowship with Him.

FOR THOSE I LOVE

I've written this for those I love
And for those who loved me, too.
I've left this world for a better place,
No need for you to feel blue.
I must admit to everyone,
Especially those who knew me best;
I wasn't worthy of this gift from God,
For much of my life was such a mess.
I'm begging you to get down on your knees
And thank God for what he has done.
Giving life to me throughout eternity
By sacrificing his only begotten Son.
God actually sacrificed Himself,
Feeling all the agonizing pain.
For the Father, the Son, and the Holy Ghost
Are all one in the same.
While on your knees, thanking him for me,
Realizing his Word is true,
Praise and thank Him for yourself,
For he also suffered and died for you.
When you put your faith in Lord Jesus,
Thankful He died for your sins,
And believing He arose on the third day,
In God's eyes you're fully cleansed.
All must stand before Him some day,
And He will speak directly to you.
I hope and pray you don't hear Him say:
"Depart from me, I never knew you."

I WAS NAMED RIGHT

I'm often asked, "Are you saved?"
My reply: "I truly like to think so."
Then eyes open wide and lower jaws drop,
Asking, "You mean that you don't know?
If you were saved, you'd know for sure,
The Bible states that plain as day.
Can I give you a flier that will show you how?"
I smile, take it, and go on my way.
I've been given similar fliers all of my life,
I've even passed them out to others.
But I've run into a big problem here,
Can you help me, sisters and brothers?
I'm probably not the only one
Who fits into the category
Who want to believe their "Good Book"
And hope to make it into "Glory."
There have been different "Good Books" written,
And I mean more than a few.
And followers of each know positively
What their "Good Book" says, is true.
Some, who know for sure, must be wrong.
Many believers are running off track.
But they're still positive and know for certain
Just what to do, and how to act.
I believe in the old King James Bible,
That's what I've been taught to believe.
I thank God when I pray, nearly every day
For shedding His blood - for me.
I believe that Jesus Christ has paid for my sins,
In my "Good Book" He made that promise.
Sometimes I wonder if I'm being taught right,
I must be a "Doubting Thomas."

A DREAM I MUST SHARE

I have a dream that I must share:
It's a giant pair of folded hands,
Huge and scarred from nail wounds,
Too big for a mortal man's.
They open up for me to see,
In a very special way -
Dad and Mom, both in one palm,
No sound, but I hear them pray
For my siblings and me and our whole family,
That all of us would be saved.
We'd be together again, in the place without sin,
And no more sorrow of dying and graves.
When I awake, I vividly remember my dream,
Kneel down and humbly bow
To thank Jesus for his great sacrifice,
So we can know we're in good hands, now.

WHAT LIFE HERE ON EARTH IS ABOUT

I no longer question how the Good Lord works
To show what life here on earth is about.
I managed to veer so far off the path
That he offered to straighten me out.
He permitted me to do whatever I wanted,
Trusting I would learn from my mistakes.
But somehow bad habits took over my life,
And a drugged up body just quakes.
Eventually realizing I was out of control
And hurting both family and friends,
I tried to quit, but couldn't dig out of this pit,
Addiction doesn't care who it offends.
When loved ones try to help or intervene,
It goes over like a lead balloon.
All anyone can do is pray for you,
Asking the Good Lord to help out soon!
When He decided to answer my loved one's prayers,
He took charge with real concern;
Knowing a few years in prison was needed
For me to dry up, think and learn.
With a clear mind and plenty of time
I can see the Good Lord does know best.
I wouldn't have kicked this habit at home,
And being hooked on drugs is a mess.
Lord, I now want to tell others of You,
Both in here and when I get out.
My life has a real purpose now,
And I know what life here on earth is about.

YOU'RE NOT TO BLAME

When the preacher spits out his sermon,
You feel he's speaking directly to you.
But the fact is, it's the preacher's biz,
To hit home with more than a few.
Most of us live similar type lives,
So it's easy for us to relate
To whatever the reverend is hitting on;
We all have secrets not up for debate.
It's easy to tell, you're giving yourself hell,
With the weight of the world on your shoulders.
I wish you would lighten up on yourself
And let go of some of these boulders.
You've been told that God is punishing you
Whenever things seem to go wrong.
But tough times happen to all of us,
And that's when you've got to be strong.
You did nothing but cry yesterday
When you found out your son must go to Iraq.
I fear you won't be able to handle it
If he doesn't come safely back.
There are no guarantees for any of us,
We just hope and pray for the best.
Chances are he'll come home a better man
After surviving this challenging test.
But if he doesn't - it's not your fault,
And you can't hold yourself to blame.
Tragedies happen - no matter what we do,
And life goes on just the same.
The Bible, when used, is often abused;
So many different beliefs - gee whiz!
Your streak of bad luck isn't punishment from God,
And you shouldn't have been told that it is.
Things go wrong, then work out for the best.
We must trust the Big Guy upstairs.
His almighty plan, we may not understand,
We just ask for His help in our prayers.

LITTLE KIDS AND CHRISTMAS

I told the kids of Santa Claus,
As we would decorate the tree,
And hang stockings from the mantel,
And giggle playfully.
He brings lots of toys to little girls and boys,
As long as they've been good.
But it's so sad when they've been bad,
They get a lump of coal or wood.
Now we must not forget what Christmas is
While we laugh and play.
The reason we should be so happy:
It's our Savior, Jesus Christ's birthday.
So let's say our prayers to Jesus
Before we go to sleep.
We'll ask Him to guide and direct us,
Our souls are His to keep.
We'll thank Him for all He does for us
While we're asleep or awake.
And if we should die before the morrow,
We pray our souls for Him to take.
These little ones grow up so fast,
And yes, they're very smart.
I would never intentionally hurt any of them,
But I broke my little girl's heart.
She was absolutely devastated.
She couldn't help but cry
When she found out Santa Claus
Was just a great big lie.
Now I'm feel I'm being punished,
Though I may have been spared the rod.
But I can see, because of me
My kids might think there's no God.

WHO'S A RUNNIN' THIS SHOW, ANYHOW?

WHO TO BELIEVE?

Should I take from the news my political views?
The media interprets what's happened or said.
Depending on who I listen to,
Blue might turn out to be red.
A democracy might work properly,
If one could trust the media news.
But reports can vary substantially;
Different eyes take different views.
It would be so nice if the truth could suffice,
Without being changed, added to or deleted.
But they like to sway you toward their opinions
And the truth is not always repeated.
An example is yesterday's baseball game:
In the seventh inning of play,
The score was tied and the bases were full,
As Griffey hits, I heard Brennaman say,
"It's a pop up." With little enthusiasm,
But he got excited when it fell in for a hit.
Two runs scored and the Reds went ahead,
But look how the media told it:
Early this morning on the radio,
They used their uncanny ability to contrive,
And changed the "pop up" that luckily fell in,
To Junior's game winning "line drive."
Countries everywhere honor their soldiers
Who died for what they believed.
And many we cherished fought hard and perished
Just because they were deceived.

COMMON SENSE

When I was a young lad growing up,
I'd hear old-timers complain:
"The end of the world is just around the corner,
Our government leaders must be insane.
I'm not worried about myself,
It's for my kids and grandkids I fear."
I asked my dad about these thoughts,
"Is the end of the world really near?"
"Son, I've heard this said all of my life,
No one knows when that day will be.
We've learned what to do in Sunday School;
We won't worry, but we're ready to see."
I guess my age must be showing,
As youngsters now hear me complain:
Our government leaders have their heads up their butts,
They don't even try to hide their shame.
Our forefathers would roll over in their graves,
Those who won us our independence,
Knowing our leaders voted in a bill that none of them read.
What's happened to our common sense?
Letting a speed reader mumble through it
Because it must be passed today;
Turning an encyclopedia sized bill into law,
Not even knowing what it has to say.
How do they come up with these hair-brained ideas?
We need some common sense leaders, for sure.
Passing laws with speed is not what we need.
Common sense isn't that common, anymore.
I'm not so worried about myself,
It's for my kids and grandkids I fear.
Borrowing trillions to bail out failing banks and businesses,
The end of the world must be near.

WHO IS OUR GOVERNMENT
WORKING FOR?

I once worked for Cincinnati Milacron,
The largest machine tool builder worldwide.
But they recently filed for bankruptcy,
And it was our government that caused their slide.
I worked in the Machine Tool Group Order Department,
I wrote the "Daily Report of New Business."
I heard daily from department heads, salesmen and execs.
I guess I would be an "eye witness."
I might hear complaints from any of them
About government pulling us under:
"They just won't bend, and they'll cause our end;
Why they continue this crap makes me wonder."
It might take a year and a half to build a machine
Needed by the aircraft industry.
But Milacron couldn't begin building until it was sold
Because of our taxation ministry.
We couldn't build anything to have in stock
Since we'd be taxed on it at the end of the year.
These machines had values of really big bucks,
To build and not sell quickly was too big a fear.
If Boeing needed a five-axis gantry type profiling machine,
They wouldn't wait seventy eight weeks to get it.
They would buy from a company that had one in stock
From a country whose government would permit it.
The incentives our businesses receive today
Are for building plants somewhere else.
Our leaders, elected to speak for us,
Get voted in by special interest wealth.

Tell me why foreigners get interest free loans
To build and purchase businesses in the U. S.
Heck, they're buying up everything,
No wonder we're in a mess.
Our leaders are putting us out of work,
They constantly pull us down.
A government written by the people, for the people
Is allowing the people to drown.
Who is our government working for?
The answer is rather obvious.
Yes, they'll milk us taxpayers dry,
But they're really working for lobbyists.

TRUSTEE

Webster defines "trust" as follows:
"Assured reliance on character, ability, strength and truth."
A "trustee" is "To whom something is entrusted."
Think about this - before you go to the booth.
You shouldn't have to stand over a trustee
To make sure they're doing things right.
You shouldn't be afraid of missing a meeting
Fearing, unwatched, there'll be another big plight.
Don't get me wrong, it's good to attend these meetings,
Trustees need to be hearing from you.
The more heads involved - questions rightly resolved,
And trustees will know better just what to do.
But when so called trustees pay little attention
To what the ones who elected them think,
They prove themselves unworthy of the job,
And that's why governments sometimes stink.
That's why we have elections every few years,
So our mistakes can be removed.
We can keep a "good one" right where he is
With better help to make things run smooth.
We need to be thinking about this now,
Don't go to the booth uninformed voting "wrong."
Get involved - find out what's happening now,
And Election Day - remove who doesn't belong.

GOVERNMENTS

Adolf Hitler's Nazi regime
Gave "true" Germans power without reservation.
They could do whatever they wanted to,
As long as it profited the German nation.
They considered themselves the "superior race,"
And loyalty to their race of blood
Took precedence over citizenship.
Everyone else was lower than mud.
They up and used their hatred for Jews
To devise the "Holocaust" scheme.
A government way of stealing assets
To help fund their selfish regime.
Most governments are more tactful today,
As they rob their citizens of wealth.
Dirt poor to wealthy, even the blind can see
Those in charge take care of themselves.

HOW TO WIN AN ELECTION

I know how to win an election,
And I'll explain it here to you.
I don't even vote, myself,
It's a waste of time to do.
Township, County, State or Fed,
All are crooked as a dog's hind leg.
When you're a runnin' for office,
Answer all your questions vague.
Just ramble on and hem-haw around,
Stay in the middle of the fence.
Never say "yes" or "no,"
Or "I'm for" or "I'm against."
Can't be honest and get elected.
Takes a bunch a dough to win.
When you do things right, you're not much of a fight.
You've gotta lie, cheat, steal and grin.
When in a campaign, you promise anythin',
We've all heard some famous quips.
I'm sure you remember this one:
"No new taxes! Read my lips!"
You gotta have good sponsors,
"Big money" in the know.
They'll handle all the advertisin',
They'll put on quite a show.
So, that's the way to do it,
You win at any cost.
And when you take your solemn oath,
Just keep your fingers crossed.
Then, once you're in this "country club,"
And a ridin' the "pleasure boat,"
The crooked money that got you there
Will tell you how to vote.

SUPREME COURT JUSTICES?

Our Constitution is the guideline -
Rules for our democracy to run right.
But Supreme Court Justices are placed
Often to build up one's might.
What if we were given the chance
To have this gravy job for a lifetime?
When all that is required for the opportunity
Is to help privileged others enlarge their lifeline.
Imagine being offered this honored position
For simply doing as you're told,
Raking in numerous fringe benefits
To enjoy when you're senile and old.
This offer would be very hard to turn down
Despite being more honorable than most.
Getting in the "clique" with the powerful
By merely obeying your host.
When enough Justices accept an offer like this,
Interpreting the Constitution however wanted,
And making their rulings as they've been directed,
Power will really be flaunted.
I'm not sure it's political parties anymore,
But "big money" that's running the show.
How would you like to play Monopoly
If you weren't allowed to pass "Go?"
Would you like to play against me this way?
I think you winning would be quite a feat.
If I could change the rules whenever I wanted,
I'd be pretty darned hard to beat.

THE SENATE AND THE HOUSE

I used to watch on cable TV
The Senate and the House.
They like to play their silly games
Like giant cat and mouse.
It struck me kinda funny
When the one behind the mike
Was buildin' up his argument,
A shakin' his fist to fight.
For all of us a watchin'
He's a puttin' on a show.
We think he's fightin' with his peers
But what he didn't know:
The cameraman got awfully bored
An' started shootin' 'round the room.
Just half a dozen people there,
And one of 'em had a broom.
Only three or four lawmakers there,
And hell, they were asleep!
But you hear 'em braggin' all the time
Of their attendance streak.
Well, the poor old cameraman
Lost his job for what we saw.
Both the Senate and House agreed
That they should pass a law.
They couldn't keep the media out,
Too obvious, that wouldn't be right.
So they decided they would let 'em stay
With just one camera on the mike.

You're in the Military, Now

DON'T I HAVE
THE RIGHT TO KNOW?

Sweetheart, I haven't heard from you,
And I write you most every day.
Don't you think I have the right to know?
Don't you have something to say?
This soldier has been informed
About you partying and carrying on.
Evidently, you've dropped me from the picture
Since the first day I was gone.
Don't you think of me, at all?
Don't you have an explanation?
Should my wanting to know your true feelings
Be beyond my expectations?
I thought we had something very special,
You are still very special to me.
Thinking about my love for you
Is now my one luxury.
I know it's hard to be alone,
And I know a woman needs a man.
It's not easy for either of us,
But don't you think I might understand?
You're right, I probably wouldn't have
Before I went off to war.
I've learned to appreciate what we once had,
I've grown up over here, for sure.
You're on my mind most all of the time,
Sweetheart, I still love you so.
Please, let me know just where I stand.
Don't I have the right to know?

CAN'T WAIT TO GET YOU BACK

It was a major shock to the whole family
When your Guard Unit was sent off to war.
You thought you had worries before you left,
Now gone for a year, and you have many more.
I apologize, I was never a soldier.
I don't know all you must be going through.
I have been trying to imagine
How tough it must be for you.
I hope you know your loved ones at home
Can't wait to get you back,
And help them straighten out their lives.
Without you, they're all out of whack.
Your sweetheart and kids long for you so.
Your mother's a nervous wreck.
Your dad and siblings are so proud of you,
They can't wait to hug their hero's neck.
We all pray every day for your safe return home,
And we all want you to know
How special you are - You are the "star!"
And all America must thank you so!

A SOLDIER'S WHAT IFS

Whenever I have the time to relax,
I think of my sweetheart back home.
I've been away for a year and a day.
Wondering, "what if" makes me moan.
What if she can't wait for me?
A woman needs a man to hold her.
What if I'm here another long year,
Will our desires grow any bolder?
What if I come home a different man
Than the one she fell in love with?
What if she does have a new love,
Can I accept it and rise above this?
Oh, I'll put the "what ifs" out of my mind,
I won't be a pathetic pessimist.
I'll be a good soldier and grit my teeth,
And try to make the best of this.

MY MAN

"My man" is going to Afghanistan,
And I need some comforting words from you.
When you come back this time, my dear,
You'll know that my love is true.
Back from Iraq, you discovered that
You'd lost most of what you'd been living for.
It's so terribly sad you were treated so bad
That is was inviting to go back to war.
I understand why my "big guy"
Must hurt as bad as you do.
I want to comfort
"my man" as much as I can,
Because I need your comfort, too.
For our love to grow, we must know
That you really do want to come back.
If you don't promise me this and send me a kiss,
We'll both be thrown out of whack.
A soldier needs to look forward to something;
Are you looking forward to being with me?
I'll treat "my man" the best that I can,
But you'll have to come back, to see.

A SOLDIER'S VALENTINE

Someone else may be taking you to dine.
Someone else may be giving you gifts.
Someone else may be sharing their love with you.
And right now, I'm not feeling too swift.
This soldier's heart is broken, my love,
Because I'm unable to hold you and say:
"You've been the best part of my life, sweetheart.
Happy Valentine's Day!"

THE HOMELESS SOLDIER

Drugs and/or alcohol have created the problems
For most of the homeless I've met.
These people are similar to you and me,
But they're now out where it's cold and wet.
Too often a large percentage of these
Are soldiers - survivors of war,
Who came home to discover they no longer have
What they were overseas fighting for.
The one who was thought to be their true love
Is picking up others most anywhere.
He or she, on the soldier's mind continually,
Evidently just didn't care.
Devastation like this can kill one's will,
So they try drugs or drink up their sorrow.
Wishing life could be as good as it once was,
But it gets even worse, tomorrow.
No, drugs and/or alcohol isn't the cure
For a kicked down and broken heart,
And it takes a strong soldier to get up from this,
Dust off, and make a new start.
A good soldier should realize they've given so much,
It was the lover who failed the test.
A good soldier must also learn from this
And understand finding a new love would be best.
Sober up, soldier! Be like you once were,
And you'll soon be happy again.
That "special one" will want you for who you are,
And be your "true lover" and your "best friend."

TAKING TOO MUCH FOR GRANTED

I once took a lot for granted,
Growing up in the U. S.
I now realize that numerous "good guys"
For my safety underwent much distress.
I'm only one of your "soldiers at war,"
Homesick for all I have lost.
You should know, too, what a soldier goes through;
Your freedom comes at a significant cost.
I've seen buddies die and wonder why
They were taken, instead of me.
As I stand guard, I try real hard
Not to be our next casualty.
I don't take anything for granted, anymore.
I'm thankful for each new day.
I wish that you were more thankful, too,
And understand what I'm trying to say.
Put yourself in a soldier's boots
And imagine how we feel.
Right now I'd give most everything I own
For a hot shower and a home-cooked meal.

THE "R" RATED MIND OF YOSEMITE SAM

WARNING!

The rest of these rhymes I've rated "R."
"R" for Redneck stuff.
They get pretty crude,
I don't mean to be rude,
But if you're a prude
Please stop here, for they are rough.
For you, I've gone too far.

But if you are down to earth, like me
And don't let yourself get too riled,
It might be a sin,
But I'll bet you a fin
That you'll get a grin.
Turn the page, but don't laugh out loud,
Or Prim and Proper might ask you to see.

SOME OLD GOAT

When I would see some old goat
A flirtin' with a young, good lookin' chick,
It would turn my stomach inside out;
It would actually make me sick!
But now I'm older and wiser
And beginnin' to understand.
When a woman goes through the change of life,
It's tough on her old man.
My wife don't care, anymore
For the ol' love makin' game.
When that gets taken away from me,
Well, life just ain't the same.
I feel like I'm a gonna explode
And she's dried up like a prune.
She's a sleepin' on the couch alone
And I've got to get some - soon!
What if I slip her some Viagra? -
Instead of sexual intercourse,
I'd be a buyin' back what's already mine
A goin' through a divorce.
I wrote to an older buddy of mine,
And he sent me back this letter:
I'm sorry, old friend, but it will tend
To get worse 'fore it gets any better.
You'd best not quit a dippin' your wick,
I'm a tellin' you this fer sher;
Or you'll get where that you don't care,
And dry up – Jest like her.
So if you see me a playin' 'round
With some young, good lookin' chick,
One of these days you'll understand
Why I up and made you sick.

THE NEIGHBOR'S DOG

I got up early one mornin',
I'd partied hard the night before.
Felt kinda sick at my stomach,
Just couldn't sleep any more.
I glanced out my kitchen window
And the neighbor's dog was a takin' a dump.
I slipped on my boots and ran out the door
To give him a kick in the rump.
Of course, I couldn't catch him,
But I chased him anyway.
I ran him right up to his doggy door
And thought - There'll be another day.
I'm in my briefs and combat boots,
And I feel this terrible pain.
It's a helluva time for nature to call,
But it's somethin' I can't detain.
I dropped my shorts to my ankles
And quickly squatted down.
I could feel the damp grass a ticklin' my ass
And my balls were a touchin' the ground.
I cut loose like a giant volcano,
And talk about somethin' that stinks!
Smokys, beer and hard boiled eggs,
And yes, I had too many drinks.
I'm a waddlin' around, a draggin' the ground,
Lookin' for decent sized leaves.
When to my greatest fear, what do I hear
But a feminine voice sayin' "Puh-leeze!"
The neighbor lady was up on her porch
And was a starin' at me real hard -
"I'm a teachin' that damn stupid dog of yours
To shit in his own back yard!"

OUR NEW SOFTBALL TEAM

Butch is getting up a softball team
To play on Sunday nights.
He came up with this bright idea
And he thinks we'll do alright.
There's three of us old timers,
Together with our sons.
The younger guys, in order to carry us,
Had better score lots of runs.
He says he has a sponsor
Who is willing to stand the hurt
Of having his proud company name
Printed on our team T-shirts.
He needs to know what numbers we want,
And the sizes that we wear.
I think to myself, "I'll need a large,
For the number, I don't care."
But I quickly reconsider,
For I might be set up for a laugh.
If I let him choose my number,
He'd probably pick one-half.
We like to ride each other,
Sometimes pretty hard.
I'm referred to as "the midget"
And he "the tub of lard."
We used to play a lot of ball
When we were in our prime.
He was a home run hitter,
But on defense - not worth a dime.
I've always been the little guy,
Yes, I am the runt.
I would hit the ball as hard as I could
And hear, "You're not allowed to bunt!"

So I don't need to leave the door open
For them to laugh at me all summer.
This time I'll play it really cool
And pick out my own special number.
Lets see, What number do I want?
I'll have to think a bunch.
I want to select one this time
That has significance.
I might prefer to pick double ought,
But wouldn't take it, if I could.
It seems that double ought and number one
Are for those who think they're good.
My birthday is on the twenty-fourth,
And I am fifty-two.
Seven and eleven are lucky numbers,
But with my luck, these won't do.
Two, three and twelve are craps,
Any of those would fit.
But I should be thinking positive
To change my luck a bit.
Chevy makes a small S-10
And also the S-15;
But I drive a Dodge Dakota,
So those numbers aren't too keen.
I live close to highway twenty-eight,
Nine miles from the park.
The neighbor lady wears size four,
Now, that gives me a spark.
I've thought on this for quite a while
And have wasted a lot of time.
Just make my shirt an extra large
With the number sixty-nine.

MARRIED TO A DELTA PILOT

I'm married to a Delta pilot.
My man is gone a lot.
Sometimes I wonder what he is doing
When I feel "hot to trot."
He is a very handsome man.
It would be easy for him to cheat.
Especially with a young stewardess,
You know they're all "in heat."
He will call me when he's gone,
As he hates to be alone.
I wonder how alone he is
When he hangs up the phone.
I'm with my daughters here at home.
I must keep an eye on them.
I wish I knew some sneaky way
To keep an eye on him.

PLAYING THEIR GAME

I grew up being quite naïve,
Boys and men took advantage of me.
I'd like to pass along some good advice
So you gals can plan your own strategy.
Guys can sometimes be perfect gentlemen
When they take you out to dinner.
Some know how to make all the right moves,
Making you feel like you're a winner.
You'll try to please him however you can,
Wanting to land this one for sure.
But it's a shame, when, for him it's a game,
And after he scores - he's "pure manure."
Go ahead gals and play their game,
But you must learn to play it slick;
And take the man for as much as you can,
Knowing he's thinking with his dick.

NOTICING THE HUMMINGBIRDS

This morning, as always, I'm thinking of you
When I notice the smallest of all hummingbirds.
Watching his pleasure is such a treasure
That I'm trying to put it in words.
With his little pecker, he's enjoying the nectar
Of the most beautiful flower in the garden.
It reminds me of you, and what we do
When you get my little pecker to harden.
After a while he flies off with a smile,
And alights, way up in a tree.
Could he be aching? Is his heart breaking?
Is he feeling somewhat like me?
It's wonderful to hold you, with all your beauty,
And taste those lovely lips of yours.
Then following our kiss comes absolute bliss
When we slip out of our drawers.
Sweetheart, you're the most beautiful flower,
And I'm just the wee little hummer.
Our pleasure I treasure beyond any measure -
But giving your nectar to others is a bummer.

COULDN'T TELL MY COHORTS

When I finally arrived at work
I gave the rest of my group a warning:
"I don't want to hear it, don't even ask
Why I'm so late this morning."
Couldn't tell my cohorts what happened,
The ignorant things I'd done.
For if I did, I'd never get rid
Of those jokers poking their fun.
I'd stopped at a station to fuel up,
Inserted the nozzle and started the pump,
When a terrible pain hits - I'm getting the shits,
So I hustle to the john and plop down my rump.
I immediately explode into the commode
And get blinded because of the vapor.
I feel all around, but none to be found;
I'm stranded without any paper.
I pull off my slacks and try to relax,
Flush twice then dampen my briefs.
Wash myself off with the soft cloth,
Needing to get out of this odor, for relief.
Once I got clean, I was feeling mean,
Pitched my briefs and slipped on my pants.
Marched to the attendant who listened, offended,
As I went off on one of my rants.
I soon could tell, others picked up the smell,
So I stormed right out of the door.
Jumped in my truck, started it up,
And pushed the pedal clear to the floor.
As I peeled out I heard him shout,
And saw him shaking his fist at me.
But I didn't linger, just gave him the finger,
And that was a real tragedy.

For when I stopped at a four-way stop,
After going about five miles or so,
My face got red when some lady said:
"Sir, there's something you should know."
Then she just pointed for me to see,
So I'd know she wasn't pulling a prank,
About ten feet of black gas station hose
Was hanging out of my tank.
It wasn't an easy thing to do,
Actually a heart wrenching task.
But I did take it back to the station attendant,
Apologized - and paid for my gas.

VIAGRA

An old buddy of mine got married again,
And he's puttin' his new young bride to the test.
With his Viagra balls they're usin' Niagara Falls
For their marathon love makin' nest.
Before they went on their honeymoon
He gave me a package of three to sample.
"Only take half of one," he said to me,
"Or you could be more than ample."
The next mornin' in front of the bedroom mirror,
All shriveled up and limp,
I figured that I'd better take 'em all;
I've never been one to skimp.
After a pot of coffee, the paper and puzzles,
I joined my wife on the couch for TV.
She's so into her favorite soaps,
But they do nothin' for me.
I went back into the bedroom
And flicked on the other set.
I'm more for huntin' and fishin' shows,
And "R" rated flicks, better yet.
I was watchin' Richard Gere and Julia Roberts,
A bathtub scene in "Pretty Woman,"
When I yelled with a cheer, "Come back here, dear,
I've got somethin' for you to hum on."
I guarantee that this stuff works,
But there's one thing I better mention:
Old Cecil, who'd been "at ease" for years
Was now standin' at "full attention."
She hurried to check out my excitement
And couldn't believe her eyes -
Then said, "Keep that thing away from me,"
Which caught me by surprise.

Cecil's one eye was starin' at me,
He's not one for takin' a joke.
My balls started achin' - my knees started shakin',
And I'm too old for the manual stroke.
I tried my best 'til my arms gave out
And I knew I had to have bruised him.
I was hopin' that if he ever went down,
I'd still be able to use him.
Takin' cold showers didn't help me
And the wife was still bein' a brat.
She at last came to bed, but kept her clothes on
And found a place there to hang her hat.
Believe me, I know - Viagra works,
Don't be wonderin' to yourself - would it?
Just be sure when you get the big boy up,
You've got a good place to put it!

MY FIRST COSTUME PARTY

I went to a costume party,
That was somethin' I'd never done.
But I'm sure glad I decided to go,
It was a helluva lot of fun.
It was hard to tell who anyone was,
The outfits were so good.
I was even proud of mine;
I'd made it out of wood.
I won't go into detail,
But we had a terrific host.
Plenty of food and alcohol,
And everyone made a toast.
It didn't take long to loosen up,
I just sat back to relax,
A watchin' all the carryin' on,
Enjoyin' it to the max.
When a cowgirl took me by the hand;
She was a total stranger.
Dressed all in white with a small black mask,
A most gorgeous Lone Ranger.
She led me to a bedroom
To play some rodeo.
She saddled up my face and said,
"Lie to me, Pinnochio!"

WHO INVENTED WORKIN' NIGHTS?

Who invented workin' nights?
I guess ol' Henry Ford.
He must have thought he'd have some fun
One time when he was bored.
I bet he enjoyed himself
When he saw what he had done.
Yes, he changed a lot of lives,
Especially ME, for one.
Sun-up makes me sleepy.
At dusk, I'm wide awake.
My mind and body are all screwed up,
On that, there's no mistake.
How do the wife and I get along,
With me on nights and her on days?
We pass each other to and fro,
Goin' our separate ways.
This shift has turned me upside down,
My head could be my feet.
I go to the table with a hard-on,
Go to bed cravin' somethin' to eat.
One day a week when we're both off,
We're a runnin' at different speeds.
I've reinforced the table
To hold up for my needs.
And then when I get hungry
And want to go to bed,
She knows just where to put my food
To get off while I get fed.

DON'T TAKE LIFE TOO SERIOUS

Don't take life too serious,
Treat it as one helluva joke.
It's too short to waste it a worryin',
Just give me some rum and coke.
When the shit starts a hittin' the fan,
And sure 'nuff, you know it will.
Sit back and rest, take a deep breath,
And let yourself coast downhill.
Whatever it is you're a frettin' about,
Worryin' ain't gonna fix it.
You can think much better when relaxed,
Get some rum and coke and mix it.
Life is all in how ya look at it.
I guess it's a frame of mind.
Treat it as a toy to give ya some joy,
And when ya screw up, don't try to rewind.
Make the best of whatever happens,
And take ya a good swig of rum.
Life is full of ups and downs,
But so is an orgasm.

BREAKFAST AT PERKINS

I stopped in at Perkins this mornin'
And ordered their "Tremendous Twelve,"
They thought they'd put one over on me,
But I'm smarter than the average Melve.
There were only eleven items;
I don't think they thought I could count.
They tried to short me a pancake,
But I promptly figured it out.
This ol' boy ain't no dummy,
Though I quit school when I was seven.
Even with my shoes on
I can count to eleven.
I unzipped my pants and counted "Wally."
No kiddin', this ain't no jive,
I wish he was a "Tremendous Twelve,"
But he's only a "Fabulous Five."

THE MARTIN'S PICNIC TABLE

I'm the Martin's picnic table,
And I lean agin' this tree.
I have but one request:
Just go and let me be.
Someone will always take me down
And set me in the grass.
They'll weight me down with vittles
Then plop down with their fat ass.
I mean several of them at a time,
It gets to be quite a load.
And they'll eat and talk for hours
Before they hit the road.
They try to impress each other,
Pretending they are smart,
And it's nearly always the broadest butt
That eases out the fart.
They'll do it kinda casually,
Like they're a reachin' for the butter.
Usually no one hears it,
But I can feel the putter.
The stench will float up like a cloud,
Sometimes as dense as the fog.
No one will ever own up to it,
It always gets blamed on the dog.
Once a young couple came along
Just as it was gettin' dark.
They sat right up on top of me
And then began to spark,
I didn't mind it much at first,
There was only two of them.
Neither was very heavy,
They were both rather slim.

I can't say what exactly happened,
As I don't have eyes to see.
But it wasn't very long at all
'Til they shook the hell outta me.
I guess people don't know how
To treat a piece of wood.
I would never treat them that way,
Even if I could.
Leanin' up agin' this tree
Is how I get my rest.
It's my favorite place to be,
It's here I feel my best.
Now I've told you how I feel.
So keep your grubby hands off me.
Pick another place to eat your meal,
Just let me lean agin' this tree.

THE TREE DISPUTE

The mighty Oak and the giant Elm,
Both were looking down
At the young and shapely tree below
That had grown up through the ground.
The mighty Oak said, "What do you think
Of my seedling, oh so slim?"
The giant Elm answered back,
Stating that it belonged to him.
They were arguing back and forth
When a woodpecker landed near.
They asked if he would be so kind
And fly down to see it clear.
He flew down to check it out,
And was gone for quite a while.
When he flew back with his feathers ruffled,
On his face he had a smile.
He said, "Neither of you are related,
You can't be any kin.
That's the best little piece of Ash
I've put my pecker in."

MY TOM

My Tom was the pride of the neighborhood.
He knew he was king of the road.
He'd strut when he walked, Meow! When he talked,
And plenty of wild oats he sowed.
Night after night it was fight after fight.
He definitely was no wussy.
He was on the prowl and didn't care how,
But he would end up with some pussy.
Then the neighbors complained, said I should refrain
From letting Tom cruise the town.
They were afraid their pussys would get laid,
Or their Toms might be put down.
So I had him de-clawed and also de-balled
And I brought him back home to recover.
Somehow I knew that it just wouldn't do
For Tom not to have any lover.
He would sit here at home, sit all day long.
He would only get up to go litter.
He'd look over at me, and I could see
His feelings were really bitter.
On the back of the chair, out the window he'd stare,
Reminiscing of days gone by.
And now it seems his life is just dreams.
What else can he do, but cry?
He'd sit all alone, just sit there and moan,
Thinkin' of what he'd be doin' if he could.
He'd watch those pussys walk by with their tails in the sky,
And know he couldn't do any good.
Now, he spends all his nights a watchin' the fights,
Right from the back of that chair.
He enjoys the view of those pussys, too,
But who wins them, he don't even care.

ENGAGED

Future Groom:

You tell me that you love me.
You say you need me so.
But when we're alone together,
You are always saying "no."
Would you put your arms around me?
Would you hold and squeeze me tight?
Would you tell me that you love me?
Would you not say "no" tonight?

Bride to Be:

But darling, we're not married yet,
And it would be a sin
For me to open up to you,
Where no one has ever been.
But I do love you very much,
And soon we will be wed.
And I will make it up to you
When we do get into bed.

Future Groom:

But you are so good looking,
And you get me so excited.
I don't believe I can wait that long
For us to be united.
Sweetheart, everyone sins,
That's why there is repentin'.
Could you at least do for me
What Monica did for Clinton?

Bride to Be:

Maybe you're right, we are engaged,
And the wedding isn't 'til summer.
I guess there wouldn't be any harm
In me giving you a hummer.
I would still be keeping my virginity,
So I can go that far.
But I want you to know, right here and now,
There won't be no cigar!

VICES

I've always heard these are vices:
Wine, women, and song.
Any of these in moderation
Doesn't seem to be too wrong.
And what about tobacco -
Chewin' and smokin' ain't a vice?
I tried to give up all of these,
And had to pay the price.
Sure, I was a boozer,
Used to run around a lot.
Hittin' all the bars and nightclubs,
Lookin' for somethin' "hot."
You could probably call these vices,
Too much of anything is wrong.
I would smoke four packs a day -
And what's wrong with too much song?
Now my doctor's a tellin' me,
"You'd better lighten up.
Those vices of yours are a killin' you,
You drink whisky by the cup!"
"I don't think I've ever seen you
Without a drink or smoke.
And you flirt with every woman you see
And you know that ain't no joke!"
So I've been really a tryin'
To straighten up my act.
I've given up an awful lot,
And that's an actual fact.

I've decided to improve myself,
Now that I'm aware of my vice.
I've even tried to walk away
After spottin' somethin' nice.
And I love my Country Music
And old time Rock-n-Roll.
So I quit singin' in the shower;
Got my song under control.
No more drinkin', smokin' and singin' for me,
That's sure been quite a task.
But to leave those sexy gals alone -
That's just <u>too much to ask</u>!